Presenting Drama in Church

Presenting Drama in Church

Roger Grainger

EPWORTH PRESS

Grainger, Roger
    Presenting drama in church.
    1. Liturgical drama   2. Christian drama
    3. Dancing——Religious aspects——Christianity
    I. Title
    264   BV10.2

    ISBN 0-7162-0408-8

7162 0408 8

First published 1985
by Epworth Press
Room 195, 1 Central Buildings
Westminster, London SW1

Phototypeset by Input Typesetting Ltd, London
Printed in Great Britain
by Billing and Sons Ltd, Worcester

To Pamela Keily

Contents

Acknowledgments

This book has aroused a lot of interest – at least, this was the impression I received all the time I was writing it. Many people have helped me put it together, some of whom I already knew well, and some I would like to know better. I can't possibly remember everyone who has influenced the way I think and feel about the business of 'acting out the faith', and the list would be far too long even if I could. However, among those whose ideas I have borrowed – if not actually stolen – are the following: Roy Clements, John Colston, Peter Dodson, Ian England, Monica Furlong, Doreen Grainger, Cynthia Hamilton-Jones, Judith Hampshire, Jeffrey Lee, Dorothy Legg, Dick Mapletoft, Ivor Moody, Ruth and Alan Redgwick, Mark Rowbottom, Phyllis Sargan, Vivian Sharman, Murray Watts, Enid Williams and Maurice Worgan. The manuscript was typed by Ann Aliffe.

Introduction

Religious drama comes in all shapes and sizes. In a Bavarian village it is the more or less permanent preoccupation of an entire community. In the evening service at the local Methodist church it expresses a simple intention of personal dedication as sidesmen and minister stand silently, heads bowed, around the offertory plate. Year by year at a parish church in the Berkshire countryside one of the York Cycle of mystery plays draws six months hard work from several neighbouring parishes. The drama of Christian worship can be ambitious or simple, studied or spontaneous, professional or amateur. In a sense, of course, it is always amateur, because it always shows love. . . It's both difficult and inevitable, hard to leave alone, equally hard to do well. On the other hand, doing it well doesn't necessarily mean being clever about it: it really means being *devoted to it*. If you think of it as something which requires a great deal of skill you may decide not to do it at all and so miss out on a world of delight which is much nearer to hand than you ever thought.

You could say, indeed, that religious drama is something you're already doing – you do it every time you go to church, every time you sing a psalm and join together in a prayer. It's something you already know much more about than you think you do. The aim of this book is to remind people about things that are forgotten or taken for granted, as much as to inform them about new ideas, approaches and techniques in religious drama. In the same way, the plays and 'happenings' described here are meant as examples to whet your appetite rather than as models to be slavishly copied. Think and pray, then decide what *you* want to do. Always remember that the possibilities of drama as a medium for human understanding, feeling and experience are immense. If you can have a dramatic happening to celebrate Epiphany, such as the one described in this book, you can have one for Lady Day, too – or for All Saints' or the

Conversion of St Paul, or any other festival of the church. You can explore secular events as these are experienced by Christians. You can illuminate any part of any church service. You can simply enjoy doing drama in a church setting for its own sake; indeed that's really the most important thing of all. So don't let the things I describe limit your own inventiveness, but take whatever is in them for *you* and use them as circumstances allow, and the Holy Spirit leads.

1 First Stages

So you want to do a play in church? You'll forgive my jumping straight in like this, but we may as well get right down to it as soon as possible. Besides, it's that kind of an idea, isn't it? 'Let's do a play: Let's do it *in church!*' That'll make people think, it'll make them feel! We'll have them laughing at all the things they take so seriously, then we'll show them the tears behind the laughter; we'll reveal in the most dramatic and striking way the effect that people have on each other and the real, practical meaning of God's revelation, the ways in which his purposes are worked out in the ordinary and extraordinary events of life; we'll present God's challenge in ways that can't possibly be ignored or avoided. It'll all be so exciting, such a change. . .

It will certainly be a change. Every play is a voyage of discovery, a launching out upon uncharted seas. It won't always be exciting, however, because most of the time it will be sheer hard work. And in fact the excitement will come mainly from the work, from the joy of seeing something emerge which you didn't know about before – something which wasn't there before you started on the play, and *it* started on *you.*

That's probably the most important thing to remember when we're talking about plays. What happens, happens both ways; and this fact must influence our attitude to what we intend to do from the beginning. It's no use even thinking about what you are going to do with a play, what effect you intend to produce on people by putting it on in your church, until you really know something of the cost involved. The cost to *yourself,* that is. I don't mean the financial outlay (although that has to be taken into consideration, of course) but the amount of hard work that a venture like this demands: hard work measured not only in terms of time spent planning, rehearsing and performing but also in terms of self-involvement at a deep level, which can be extremely arduous, and genuine self-disclosure, which is always painful. If it isn't, then you're not really doing it!

There you are, then. It isn't only a matter of what you plan to do with and for other people. It is also, and primarily, a case of what will be happening to *you* while you're engaged in doing it. Can you cope? Are you willing to try? A really bad play – badly written, badly produced, badly acted, is an abomination. We have all suffered experiences of that kind. How can you be sure that it isn't going to happen to you, this time? The forgotten lines, the missing props, the badly painted scenery that collapses halfway through the first act. . . Do you really know what you're letting yourself in for?

All this applies to the group as a whole, of course. I'm writing about it in the singular but it's just as true in the plural. It's always as well to know the dangers inherent in any enterprise, although these things are much easier to undertake when the risks are shared. Indeed, this is extremely important. Religious theatre is always really group threatre. It is theatre about the life of the worshipping community and it emerges from that life. The rule about group theatre is that it is a theatre of sharing – not only of the final product, the play that is shared with the audience in the actual performance, but the actual making of the play, in all its details, belongs to the group and reflects the life of the group. This doesn't mean that there's no one in charge. Indeed in some of the freer forms of theatre that we shall be looking at later, firm direction is very necessary, because you have no set text to follow or playwright to interpret. But it does mean that there must be a high level of consensus within the group about its aims and objectives. For instance, no one should regard the play as simply a vehicle for his or her own talents. In group theatre, we're all in it together. We start off together and we travel together. If, and when, we fall, we all fall together. . . Individuals will have ideas, and these will be considered and discussed by the group; but even those ideas that are accepted will inevitably be changed, as they become part of the group experience and pass through the kaleidoscopic process whereby they come into contact with the personal lives of all the individuals who make up the group. The necessary authority for leadership is delegated, and consequently *accepted,* by the group itself. If this is really understood, and acted upon, it is the greatest source of strength in any theatrical venture. No one knows at which point inspiration will arrive, and to whom it will be given. It's the responsibility of anyone who has been chosen to have any kind of responsibility for the play to make sure that inspiration can work through the relationships which already exist, so that new kinds of relationships are free to emerge. If there's enough love in the group, you can't fail. By love, I mean not only mutual acceptance, but the positive celebration of one another's individual personalities, for love is a gift, not a requirement, and no amount of expertise on the part of talented people can make up for its absence. Here, as in all other areas of the church's life, there must be willingness to share. (A group which is working like this won't always be *happy*, of course. Indeed, from one point of view this kind of mutuality is the best way of making trouble for yourselves, as all sorts of hidden resentments and jealousies which are kept in check within an authoritarian atmosphere are free to come to the surface and wreak havoc with the feelings of everyone present. But it is likely to be a temporary kind of havoc, because people who feel confident enough to come out into the open and let their feelings be seen are usually confident enough to use what resources they have in the way of sympathy and understanding towards other people to make sure that this kind of upsetting episode has a creative effect in the direction of a greater ability to 'bear one another's burdens', and so grow into a deeper and more genuine attitude of loving acceptance towards the group than they had before. Usually, that is. Putting on a play is one of the most effective kinds of 'group therapy' that there is; but, like group therapy, it doesn't *always* work!)

The willingness is all; or if not quite all, then at least ninety percent of what is needed to put on a good play in a church. Certainly, it is much more important than any kind of technical skill. But it must be an informed willingness; and a good deal of the necessary information concerns emotional factors within the group itself. I shall be saying more about this later on. For the time being it's worth pointing out that it is not enough simply to look round the church and decide that it would be a good place for a play; although most churches are! It isn't even enough to make sure that the play will be adequately cast, that there are enough talented people in the congregation to ensure a sufficiently high standard of acting and production. (This may even be a bad way of starting off, in fact, because talent is the kind of thing that tends to emerge in unlikely places, as professional theatre people know!). Perhaps the most important thing of all is courage. You need the courage to look around and see what is there, and then to *use* it – and yourself – to create something genuinely corporate, which is another way of saying something personal. If it is personal to the actors and producer, it will be personal to the audience as well. And this is what really matters.

Finally, *time*. You will definitely need time to prepare. Some of the most unforgettably catastrophic experiences of church drama that I have ever endured have owed their particular awfulness to sheer lack of rehearsal. Unfortunately, this is often the fault of the clergy. For instance, some weeks before Lent begins, the Vicar decides that it would be a good idea to do a play for Easter. By the time he has rounded up a group of people willing to take part, Ash Wednesday has passed by leaving only six weeks or so to Good Friday. The play is one which impressed the Vicar when he read it. It's a literary piece, containing some sound doctrinal teaching, but cleverly put together so that the hard theology doesn't show through very much. Altogether both suitable and striking, if well done. Unfortunately, some of the cast leave after the first read-through. 'Too many lines to learn. Besides, it's a bit boring, isn't it?' Not to worry, however, because somebody knows somebody else from another parish who'll probably help out, when the play they are in at the moment has finished. Three weeks to go now, and the cast manage to squeeze in six or seven rehearsals, including the dress rehearsal. In due season the play goes on. It really isn't very good; although 'considering the time we had', it could have been a lot worse. The audience is very appreciative. One or two of them approach the Vicar after the performance and say things that show they understood what it was about (what it was *really* about, that is). This is a relief to him, because he has had doubts all through rehearsal as to the suitability of his choice. The cast hadn't seemed all that keen to begin with, and he had to admit that the play was a bit obscure in parts. But he has under-estimated his congregation – it's a habit he has – because they've really risen to the occasion. They've really enjoyed the play.

Of course they have. It's a good play, even it if is a bit self-consciously artistic, and the cast by now are beginning to have the makings of a good cast (pity they won't have an opportunity to grow into a better one!) The audience, of course, are really very good indeed – eager to support their friends in the cast, sensitive to the atmosphere which pervades this special season, hoping to discover new truth in familiar doctrines, rejoicing when they find it; you couldn't ask for a better audience. And you can't help wondering whether they didn't deserve more than they got.

In fact, what everybody deserved, the audience, the producer, particularly the actors, was more time. There should have been opportunities for discussion even before rehearsal of the play began. Actors and producer should have allowed themselves the opportunity to get to know one another better. You can't discover what is in a play until you've begun to be aware of what is in yourselves. This is where amateurs can learn so much from their professional brethren. No group starts off 'cold' in the way that these unfortunate people had to do. There is always time for exploration, both of the group and the play; talking about the play, sharing ideas about the best ways of approaching the job of presenting it, or at least commenting on the producer's ideas about this, trying to discover what was in the author's mind when he wrote it, etc. As we shall see, one of the best ways of doing this is by encouraging people to imagine situations like the ones contained in the play and extemporizing dialogue for them; another way is to experiment with different acting styles, comedy, tragedy, farce, documentary, even opera and musical comedy, in order to get away from fixed ideas about how plays like this one should always be done. As the play is unpacked so is the group itself becoming more relaxed in one another's presence, and consequently more flexible and spontaneous. Enthusiasm in the project grows as the possibilities contained in the play are gradually revealed. People begin to laugh at one another, and barriers of shyness begin to disintegrate. People's imaginations start to work even before the serious labour of rehearsal begins – and rehearsals themselves tend to be more serious and workmanlike because the actors and actresses are genuinely interested in what is going on.

All this is very important because of the effect it will have on the final product: only if the cast are really involved will they be able to secure the audience's involvement. The story which is being enacted must fascinate the people who are playing it out before it can capture the imagination of anyone who is watching it. In short, the producer must do all he can to arouse the enthusiasm of his cast for the play he has chosen. If this takes up valuable time, time which could be spent learning lines and practising moves, it can't be helped. It simply means that more time must be given to the production as a whole. More time means enough time: time for enthusiasm to grow into confidence and the freedom to use one's own personality effectively in the service of the play. If, after all this, nothing much changes, and people are still bored by what's going on – if they signal their lack of interest in the time-honoured way of standing around in groups and talking when they should be concentrating on the play – then it would be better to give the whole thing up and do something else instead. If you can't capture their interest by involving them in the process of creation, it's certainly no good getting angry and shouting or even appealing to their personal loyalty to one another and to you. A production must have something for everyone; something *new* and exciting. Nobody's impressed by a play done solely to please the Vicar!

However, there *are* other things you can do. Up to now I've been mainly talking about the kinds of play that people usually do in churches; ordinary, straightforward plays, generally of an overtly 'religious' kind. But there are alternatives to this approach, things that don't take up quite so much time and involve such a high degree of individual and corporate involvement, which can be quite remarkably effective for all that. If you can't produce a formal play – if you've tried hard and not really got very far with it – perhaps it would be better to scrap it and try something else. Religious drama is a very wide field indeed, and one that is still growing. I shall be mentioning some of the options which already exist during the course of this book. I hope to deal with one or two in some depth – mainly those which I've had some experience of. For the time being, however, it's worth remembering that your efforts up to now haven't been wasted. At the very least you have got people thinking about the possibility of using drama as a way of proclaiming the unique quality of the Christian experience. And you've got to know some of your fellow Christians much better than you did before. So, persevere. . .

Apart from time, and willing people, the thing that's needed most of all is imagination; imagination for setting appropriate goals and deciding on ways and means of achieving them. Obviously a good deal of imagination is needed for the actual staging and acting of a play, for drama is driven by this particular fuel and grinds to a halt whenever supplies run out. But creative thinking is needed from the very beginning. Before you can work on a dramatic event of any kind, you have to decide what kind of event it is that you want!

Perhaps the content may seem straightforward enough. You're clear about what kind of message you want to deliver, what kind of story you'd like to tell. At least, this seems a reasonable assumption to make in the case of religious drama. Deciding exactly what form your message will take is more difficult. Will it be a rehearsed piece of theatre, a dramatic 'happening' which depends on improvization, a symbolic ritual within the setting of an act of worship, a dialogue sermon, or what? There are so many alternatives. You have to use your imagination to decide which would be best. Is one form exactly right for your situation? Could you contrive a fascinating kind of hybrid, using several forms, either simultaneously or in juxtaposition with one another? If you did, would the result be delightful, or would it be simply a mess? Or could you really be inventive, really courageous, and create an entirely new kind of religious drama reflecting the uniqueness of your own Christian experience with particular people in a particular place? You might find, if you did this, that surprising things began to happen. Starting from the things you are familiar with and the people you know can turn out to be the best plan of action of all. You could have gone further and fared worse! Some of the most exciting drama of the modern theatre has been built on this 'documentary' kind of approach. It takes courage to contrive the formal shape of a play yourself, but it is courage well applied. I've yet to see a play of this kind which failed to come across, however ramshackle its construction. This is because, in all art and particularly the drama, content and form are interdependent. If the content, the story that is, is really true, really evocative in its ability to reach our minds and hearts to become part of our experience, the form will somehow emerge. In feeling it, we ourselves give it form. Similarly, if the way that things have been put together is sensitive enough, so that it chimes with the reality it aims to represent, it ends up by influencing that reality, in order to make it even more real. It allows it to express a truth which we can recognize as universal, rather than particular, and so becomes a symbol, instead of simply an example.

But you have to decide. If you feel that you must 'play safe' there are several more orthodox ways of going about things. You should be warned, though, that drama being drama, things won't ever turn out exactly as you planned. They never do. The stuff of even the most ordinary play is fissionable material. Plays take over actors and actors transform plays. Somebody else's nativity drama, a book taken from a library shelf or borrowed from a neighbouring church, a play specially commissioned or one rescued from a previous production dating back thirty or forty years inevitably becomes *your* play when you start to work on it; your difficulties, your triumphs, your own particular message, the 'tongue wherein you were born'. All this doesn't actually help you make up your mind, of course. And in fact it's much better not to try to do it by yourself, but to take the problem of choosing something appropriate, interesting and exciting to the group who have offered to participate. After all, they are going to be involved in whatever happens, so they ought to be in at the start of things. If you haven't got such a group, then you must go about getting one. Once you have some people to work with, you might try the time-honoured technique of 'brain-storming'. The object of this is to generate a great many ideas on a particular subject in a reasonably short time. You place a black-board at one end of the room and ask for ideas. Then you write on it every suggestion that crops up without comment, taking care not to discard anything, however 'far-out' it may seem. (It's a good idea to keep your own suggestions back until someone else has contributed and so avoid the implication that you yourself already know exactly what kind of thing will eventually take place. Even if you don't, it will look as though you do if you plunge in straight away.) Once the ideas start coming, they usually flow quite rapidly. Then equally suddenly, everybody 'dries up' and no one can think of anything else to add to the list. At this point you can start to discuss the ideas one by one, asking people to say whether they find each one attractive, and if they think it's practicable or not. This tends to shorten the original list, but adds value and interest to the remaining suggestions as some of the characteristics of the ideas that have been excluded become attached to them. In this way it's possible to achieve a kind of synthesis of people's ideas and attitudes, and frequently something entirely new emerges. This only happens so long as the people present feel that their own suggestion has been properly considered. At least it was worth writing down! 'Brain-storming' frees group problem-solving from competitiveness, making it a corporate exercise whose goal is the problem itself rather than the satisfaction of having impressed everyone present by having come up with the 'right' answer. And even if you are convinced that you've had a brilliant idea yourself, its superiority will be made even more evident when it is set alongside alternative suggestions. If it isn't, then drop it. It wasn't as good as you thought!

If you can't come up with anything, or you can't agree but still want to do something, or you really feel you don't know enough about it, then seek outside help. You can do this earlier on, of course, but this decision is probably better coming from the group too.

The best place to look for advice and assistance is to the Religious Drama Association of Great Britain, usually called RADIUS. This is a national body, which works with all the Christian churches, with the professional theatre and with various voluntary organizations, helping local Christian congregations and creative groups towards a deeper understanding of the value of all kinds of drama, and supplying the background of direction and technical advice needed to reach a workmanlike standard for the presentation of plays and dramatic happenings. In its own words, 'RADIUS exists to encourage drama which illuminates the human condition. It believes that the central point of reference for this purpose is Jesus Christ; but it recognizes that many contemporary dramatists do not share this view and welcomes all attempts to create a true dialogue between men in their social relationships, believing that this will make clearer man's relationship with God.' Although founded over fifty years ago, RADIUS has kept its finger on the pulse of change throughout its fascinating career, and has been a way of using change – change in society, in church and parish life, and in the theatre itself – to explore the drama as a vital medium for expressing religious experience. Nowadays it is involved in worship and the arts, in dance-drama and religious education. It has an extensive, and very imaginative, library, and classified catalogues of plays, sketches and musical shows are available for local groups, and an advice service which provides invaluable help for the undecided and the inexperienced. RADIUS always welcomes a challenge and goes out of its way to encourage new initiatives. Among the other benefits it offers are a yearly summer school, lasting eight days, and providing a range of instruction at the hands of professional teachers in all aspects of drama, including speech, movement, music, design and production; a professional touring company which visits church communities through Britain, not only to present plays but also, and equally importantly, to foster interest in drama as a practical way of understanding life and exploring religious truth; and a very useful magazine which appears twice a year. This contains articles on the theory of religious drama as well as accounts of actual ventures within the field. The latter are always fascinating to read about, and set the imagination working in order to discover ways in which they, or similar ideas, could be adapted to answer the needs and exploit the opportunities present in one's own unique church situation. Altogether, RADIUS is too good a resource to ignore; and ministers and congregations who feel confident enough to choose their own kind of drama would be well advised to make use of at least some of the facilities it provides, if only as a source of encouragement when they meet the difficulties and encounter the crises that lie in the path of every venture into the drama; hazards which, when it comes down to it, can only really be overcome by the group itself as it works through its own problems to make its own discoveries.

Note

The address of RADIUS is St Paul's Church, Covent Garden, Bedford Street, London WC2E 9ED. Some very good ideas about the simple use of drama in order to present biblical ideas with maximum clarity and impact are to be found in Janet and Steve Stickley, *Using the Bible in Drama,* Bible Society 1980.

2 Options

There are four main alternatives open to anybody who is interested in putting plays on in church:

Firstly, *someone can perform a play for you,* either one that they have written themselves, or one that somebody else has written for them. (By which I mean a play specially commissioned, or one belonging to the repertoire of published plays.) The degree to which this will be *your* play will depend to a large extent on how well they do it. Any play that captures the imagination of the audience is at least partly the audience's play, because theatre depends upon this kind of mutual co-operation, and can't every really do without it.

Secondly, *you yourselves can perform someone else's play* – that is, a play written by someone else. This is what usually happens, of course. The play begins as someone else's, and ends up being very much yours as well. You're able to make it your play as well as the author's by working hard at it in the ways I shall be describing in this book.

Thirdly, *you can make your own play out of someone else's 'raw material'.* This is difficult to do, but always immensely rewarding. It requires the same kind of concentration on the material at hand as is needed for the second option, coupled with the artistic imagination essential for giving the material the right kind of dramatic shape. (This may seem a bit off-putting, but don't be discouraged. Given the opportunity a lot of people end up surprising themselves. They never realized they were creative before!)

Fourthly, *you can make your own play from material that is genuinely your own,* by extemporizing your own dramas and fashioning the result into theatre. This follows on from the third method, but at the same time it is the most basic theatre of all. It is certainly the most challenging approach, and perhaps the most satisfying one. We shall be looking at it in detail in chapter 4.

Meanwhile, the main purpose of this chapter is to serve as an introduction to the various ways of approaching the fascinating business of putting a play on in church.

1.   Plays performed by visiting companies in your church

During the last fifty years several theatre groups have followed in the footsteps of Martin Brown's Pilgrim Players who were associated in the 1930s and 40s with performing plays of high literary merit, often with a powerful religious and philosophical character (e.g. T. S. Eliot's *Murder in the Cathedral* and work by Charles Williams, Norman Nicholson and Christopher Fry). The work done by Pamela Keily in Sheffield and later in Wakefield, Manchester and Ripon maintained the high professional standards of the Pilgrim Players, using amateur actors and actresses. I have heard recently of groups of parishes and local congregations which have set out to pool their resources and produce plays of a high enough standard to be taken on tour and performed in other people's churches. A notable example is the East Kent Company, Group 81. The movement, I'm glad to say, seems to be growing. The original impetus came from a desire to revive the mediaeval tradition of poetic drama, and some of the productions mounted by visiting companies in local churches are still well within the mystery tradition, even if they aren't actually written in verse. That is, they aim at imaginative involvement rather than theological polemics. Other companies, some professional, some amateur, work in a more flexible way, with varying degrees of success. Among the professionals, Riding Lights and Theatre Roundabout are outstanding. This is a difficult area for actors and directors who aren't highly skilled and experienced. There's a tendency for such entertainments to be so loosely constructed as to lack the driving force of a single over-riding idea, something to give them a recognizable artistic shape. This is a pity, because ideas are what this kind of theatre is all about. At its best, modern street-theatre has a knock-about spontaneity and rough-and-tumble humour inherited from the tradition of folk theatre, the mummer's plays which still draw audiences at local fêtes and country fairs. It doesn't just hit you between the eyes with its ideas, but slips them under your guard while you're busy laughing at the absurd way in which they're being presented. Unfortunately there is a tendency for this kind of 'rough theatre' to lose some of its impact when you bring it indoors and present it in church. I have seen examples of the use of this technique by travelling companies dedicated to the use of satire for the purpose of making serious points about the Christian faith. Because of their determination to avoid any of the techniques associated with 'straight' theatre, the result tended to be too diffuse to be really effective – a series of music-hall sketches strung one after the other until every controversial issue in the life of the church had been tackled and all possible attitudes to the faith debunked. The continual changes of style which work so well in street theatre, where you have to keep seizing the attention of people passing by, can be very wearing to a captive audience who are in no position to move on when they have had enough. From this point of view, the company I mentioned earlier, Riding Lights, the main heirs to the 'morality' traditions of explicit theatre, set an excellent example. Not only is their method of presentation highly disciplined, but their material is never too long. Their sketches concentrate on making a single point as well as possible.

The question of the length of plays presented in churches is very important. A play or sketch which is supposed to take the place of a sermon should be no longer than a sermon. That is, it shouldn't ever last for more than half an hour at the very outside. I myself have been on tour with plays lasting longer than this which the priest or minister had tried to squeeze in as part of the usual evening service. When we reached the second lesson, the congregation would invariably start to get restless, knowing that the main business of the evening hadn't even started yet. I make no apology for putting it like this. People tend to talk about watching a play as if it were an easier thing to do than it is. And yet, subconsciously at least, they realize that it calls for a special kind of concentration. I don't mean that it takes more concentration than worship does, just that it's a different kind of mental activity. In order to enjoy a play, you have to change gear mentally and start using your imagination in a different kind of way. This isn't always an easy thing to do three-quarters of the way through a service – which is why people don't seem to be all that keen on your performance when you start and it takes them so long to warm up and enjoy themeselves. Despite a common origin, plays and church services aren't the same kind of thing at all; and people who invite visiting companies to perform in their churches would do well to remember this. Most plays are written to stand on their own. The play makes its own statement and if it needs any kind of introduction or postscript it looks after such matters itself, using specific theatrical conventions to do so. Extra-theatrical additions should be kept to a bare minimum, and really ought to be postponed until the play has finished, when prayers can be said both silently and corporately and a hymn sung. Of course, the play can, and should, be discussed, but on a later occasion. Some kinds of theatre lead naturally into a discussion between actors and audience. The theatre of the imagination, however, needs time for its message to take hold. It may be a matter of days, or even weeks, before we really get the point of a play which has moved us a great deal. You don't have to understand a play completely in order to enjoy it. As I said, plays are things to be worked on, for the audience as well as the cast. If you're fascinated by what you've been involved in, you'll take it away with you and wait for it to speak to you in its own time. If you're not interested at this level, no amount of discussion is going to help, and you may as well forget it.

This being the case, it's much better to avoid the impulse to say a few words of explanation before the play begins. However well meant, this almost always has the effect of putting people off. If it doesn't discourage the audience, it tends to annoy the actors, who want their performance to be allowed to speak for itself. In short, the rule here is the same as everywhere else: what's needed is courage. Just as you must have it to do a play yourself, so you need it to let someone else do one in your church. Above all, the thing you should resist is the temptation to take refuge in unsatisfactory kinds of compromise. If people object to any interference with the normal Sunday service, and you don't want to offend them, choose another time and encourage the congregation to come and see the play then. Some kinds of drama fit easily into ordinary church worship; but if the kind of play offered to you doesn't, then for goodness sake don't try and make it. If you do, everybody will be unhappy – you, the congregation, and the visiting players.

2.   *Performing plays written by other people*

Most plays done in churches fall into this category. Different kinds of play require different kinds – and degrees – of skill. Musical plays and 'rock operas' obviously demand some musical skill as well as enthusiasm and 'attack'. In a play which depends mainly on emotional realism, there's a good chance that a comparatively unskilled performer who has become imaginatively involved in the dramatic situation within the play, so that he or she is actually feeling the emotions of the character concerned, will manage to communicate something of this to the audience. On the other hand a play which aims at a direct relationship between audience and actor without the interposition of a carefully and realistically drawn character for both sides to identify with needs a much more practical approach. For amateur companies I would definitely recommend the first kind of play. (I also happen to think that this is what theatre is all about!)

As to whether a play written by a professional playwright is to be preferred to one specially written by a member of the congregation, I'm not at all sure. Sometimes this kind of challenge produces surprising results; sometimes, too, the people we take for granted turn out to be remarkably creative. At the time of writing, there seem to be a remarkable number of clergy playwrights around. I've come across examples in Yorkshire, Lincolnshire, Staffordshire and Sussex, and there are probably many more that I've not heard about yet. But whoever wrote the play, our attitude to the author should be one of respect; respect for the meaning it enshrines, at the deepest level of which we're capable, respect for his aims and intentions in writing it, and respect for his rights. Which aren't only financial (although of course they may be this, too), but also include more personal ones, such as the right to be informed that we're putting the play on, and to be invited along to the performance. (When I say *his* I do of course mean *her* as well. I realize that plays aren't only written by men!) If you're working from a play script you have a very strong advantage, in that you have the playwright's conception to start from. This means that you've always got someone to consult, not only about the lines you're supposed to say, but about the attitude of mind you're intended to be in when you say them. To a large extent this motivation arises from the action of the play, the things that happen to you in the play, the kind of person you turn out to be, but it doesn't only depend on this. Apart from the plot, the characters and the dialogue, the playwright brings at least two other vital contributions to the play: firstly, he brings his artistic skill; secondly, he contributes his own personal world-view. (It's worth remembering, of course, that neither of these is entirely his own. To a large extent he has picked them up from other people.

All the same he has certainly made them his own, fashioning them within the play into something uniquely personal.)

The Oxford Dictionary defines 'art' as 'a skill in which mind and imagination are concerned'. It also refers to such words as 'knack', 'cunning' and 'stratagem'. For a play to come across as a piece of theatre it has to be skilfully put together. Like any other kind of persuasive form of personal communication it needs to be skilfully argued. This doesn't mean that the characters have to be exceedingly verbose or emotionally forthcoming. Even all of Shakespeare's don't fit that description! But it does mean that the play's construction must itself be eloquent; that it must use the various ploys and devices that we ourselves use when we want to get a point across in as convincing a way as possible. When we want to seize and hold the attention of someone we're talking to we make use of humour, tenderness, satire, pathos, all sorts of varied approaches. We use shock tactics to bring home a point, or we deliberately delay our effects. Most of all, we rely on *variety* and on *contrast*.

It goes without saying that playwrights do all these things; and do them much better than we do. A superlative artist-technician like Shakespeare never ceases to fascinate his audience – and his players, too – with the ways in which he uses the difference between contrasting kinds or intensities of human feelings in order to heighten his emotional effects. The example that springs immediately to mind here is the famous incident of the Porter in *Macbeth,* where tragedy is made unbearably intense by the riotous implosion of ribaldry at the moment when it is least expected and most shockingly inappropriate. And yet, of course, it isn't – for the outrageousness of the juxtaposition underlines the horror of what has happened in a way that literally takes our breath away. 'Confusion now hath made his masterpiece!' Not every playwright is Shakespeare, of course. But all dramatists give us something definite to start from, something that has a kind of artistic shape and uses the basic artistic means of correspondence and contrast, continuity and interruption, ebb and flow, in order to achieve the kind of balance of ideas and impressions which characterizes a work of art. Certainly it's possible to do this kind of thing for oneself, and if we are going to be really courageous and try to put our own play together, then we shall have to have a go at doing it. All the same, we may as well be honest and admit straight away that we aren't likely to be as good at it as, say, Ibsen or Chekov. And the fact remains that to do their best work actors need a good play to get their teeth into. A good play in this sense means one that demands a leap of the imagination from the people whose job it is to bring it alive for the audience. You need something to work on, preferably something that isn't too much like you yourself: an alien world that you can struggle to make your own. Not entirely foreign, of course, because you need to recognize your own humanity in the men and women you meet within the play; but not too familiar, either, or nothing new can happen, nothing original can be created. Something has to become you, and that takes effort and concentration.

There are two ways of achieving this kind of knowledge of 'the world of the play'. First of all, it's necessary to study the play itself, the play as it stands, without any kind of historical background, any *outside* knowledge we may possess or acquire about the lives, experiences, attitudes or opinions of authors or characters. In order to study a text adequately it isn't enough to learn the lines. You have to learn the shape of the action, too. By which I mean the things that happen in it, from scene to scene (yes, even the scenes that your character doesn't appear in!). Why has the playwright arranged things in this particular order? What very precise point is he trying to make? How would the play's final impact have differed if he had done something else, perhaps done the thing we'd have expected him to do? And what about this particular line? I can't think why my character's got it at all – it just doesn't seem to make sense. I'm sure it's a mistake, perhaps it's really *your* line! It would be much easier if we could wriggle out of the difficulties which beset us when we're faced with the task of performing someone else's play by simply re-arranging it in conformity with our own ideas and preferences. It seems to me that it's part of the basic morality of theatre that we shouldn't allow ourselves to give in to this kind of temptation. It's a shocking thing when a play is produced in a way which runs directly counter to its playwright's intention, so that the original message is distorted out of all recognition. I once saw a production of the Last Judgment, from the Towneley Cycle of Mystery plays, in which Christ was portrayed as performing his final duties with a nauseating mixture of malevolence and hilarity. I shall never forget the effect this had. It was almost enough to put one off the theatre for good. Nevertheless, this is the kind of thing that frequently happens with productions of classical plays. Directors frequently know better than authors. And yet it is the creative challenge of coming face to face with someone else's own distinctive, personal, unique world that brings our dramatic heritage to life time and time again, as we use a work of art to recreate a private vision and a public universe.

The second way in which we come into contact with the life which avails us in somebody else's play is by learning as much as we can about the author and the society he lived in. By studying his other work and making ourselves familiar with the works of art created by his contemporaries – by generally immersing ourselves in the intellectual and spiritual atmosphere of his time and place – we begin to be able to glimpse something of life as he himself saw it, and consequently as he imagined his characters seeing it. These two things, the interior relationships between events and people taking place within the action itself, which is the world the play sets out to reveal to us, and the personal attitudes, experiences, assumptions and expectations of the playwright, the world that he brought to the action in the first place, provide us with endless opportunities for study and speculation. As long as we go on working on a play that we are genuinely interested in we continue to be surprised by it. Perhaps the following story may make both of these points a little clearer:

I once played the part of the Earl of Salisbury in *Henry V*. This was during the 1962 Old Vic season, my first with the company, and one I'm not likely to forget. Why this play sticks in my memory so firmly is because of one particular scene, the celebrated one in which the English army learns the news of the outcome of the battle of Agincourt: 'Now, herald – are the dead numbered?' This scene begins with a comic interlude involving Fluellen and King Henry when the former discovers that the anonymous soldier with whom he has been quarrelling during the night watch was in fact the king himself. It is into the middle of this semi-farcical situation that the English herald comes bearing his list of the newly slaughtered. The Englishmen listen in silence as they hear the names read out: 'This note doth tell me of ten thousand French / That in the field lie slain. . .' It's a long list and contains the flower of French chivalry, men famous throughout Europe, admired and respected by their English counterparts (including Salisbury!) and often related to them by marriage or actually by blood: 'Here was a royal fellowship of death.' But if this is the toll of the losses that the French have suffered, what about the English dead? Night after night for a whole season we stood on that immense stage in shocked silence, hardly daring to let ourselves hear what the herald would say next. For if France had bought victory at such a cost – and we had no doubt at all at this point that it was the French who had won, how could it be otherwise? – what would the price of our own defeat be? The herald spoke again: 'Edward, Duke of York, the Earl of Suffolk, Sir Richard Kelly, Davy Gam, Esquire.' And we were swept, in the course of three lines, from the misery of fear and grief – fear for ourselves, grief for the fate of our beloved enemies – through stunned unbelief into rapturous relief: 'Tis wonderful.'

I can honestly say that I have never been made to feel so many different emotions in the course of so few lines, and with such devastating impact. Every time we played that scene, this amazing reversal of feeling brought tears to my eyes. You see, it wasn't so much the shortness of the English list as the fact that before the herald could stop speaking we were already set free: 'Davy Gam, *Esquire.*' Lists of casualties were always read out in order of rank! *There couldn't be anyone else!* The unbelievable fact that we had only lost four of our friends came crashing down on us every time we played the scene, always managing somehow to catch us unprepared. If we hadn't known this, the effect on our feelings wouldn't have been anything like so powerful. We wouldn't have known it, of course, if we hadn't set about learning as much about the play as we possibly could while we were rehearsing it. Certainly the wonderful contrast of feelings would have come across to the audience without this particular bit of inside information, because Shakespeare has arranged the action in a way that sets comedy, tragedy and joyful celebration cheek by jowl within the very same scene. But it would never have worked so reliably with us if we hadn't taken the effort to do our homework properly. After all, like most people, we already knew the story before beginning rehearsals, and we had to perform the play more than fifty times before the season was over. Now we had discovered the secret of keeping the feeling fresh we had very little difficulty in convincing the audience that it was all happening for the first time. The secret lay in the way that, once you know about Davy Gam and his significance, personal realization of deliverance arrives a mere pulse, a split second, before the 'official' news of victory, catching the mind unprepared, slipping under the defences that it erects to preserve itself from information it isn't ready to digest.

There's no substitute, then, for really working on the script. You don't do this in order to see what you can put into it, but what you can take from it. Sometimes, if you're working with a brilliant playwright like Shakespeare, there's so much in a scene that the actor's main job is to avoid getting in the way of what the author is saying. One of the very first things an actor must learn is how to let the text speak for itself. You don't need a special way of saying things or moving about the stage. Even if you manage to learn a lot of 'technique' so that you walk and talk 'like a professional' your aim still remains the same, to communicate the playwright's intention to the audience. It's an unfortunate fact that actors' 'technique' often serves exactly the opposite purpose. In other words, it only succeeds in drawing attention to his or her own – perfectly natural – desire to stand out from the rest of the cast as a 'good actor'. This is understandable, but it doesn't help the play very much, and serves the author very badly indeed. Real technique, the kind it's worth working towards, is less self-conscious than this. It consists in learning how to lose oneself in the play. 'Listen to what he says to you and reply to it. It's as simple as that!' This was said to me when I had recently left drama school, and was still exceedingly proud of 'what I could do with a part'. What I still had to learn was how to concentrate on letting a part do things to me, instead: allowing an author to use me in order to communicate his message to an audience. His, not mine.

Producer and cast work on the text together, showing respect for one another's views, deferring to the intentions of the playwright when these are obvious, and working towards some kind of a consensus about how to proceed when they aren't. I say 'some kind of consensus' because it is certainly important that everyone should understand that the final word rests with the producer. This doesn't mean, however, that there shouldn't be discussion of differing interpretations. Certainly the producer must always make sure that the reasons behind his decisions are fully understood. Too often, especially in amateur productions, the producer arrives for the first rehearsal with the whole play already sewn up in advance. Just as the cast must pay heed to the producer, so the producer must attend to the ideas, feelings and intuitions of his cast. The rules are straightforward enough: Listen to one another; listen most of all to the playwright; concentrate on your role, letting it work on you and in you; approach the character you have to play with a certain amount of humility, thinking about him or her as much as you can as you go through the day, trying to think *as* him or her. Do this quietly and gradually, without rushing, so that it becomes habitual. In this way you'll find your character gradually 'taking over' on one level of consciousness. (Don't worry, the process won't get out of hand. Instead you'll simply discover that the person is there when you want him or her.) One thing you must try never to do is to adopt a role from the outside by practising a set of mannerisms – a particular way of walking, standing or talking that you think would be suitable for a person like that. If these characteristics arise naturally from the deepening relationship between you and your role, well and good; but never try and force them. Work from the inside, not the outside. In the business of creating a character patience is much more useful than inventiveness. In any case, the imagination works better when you don't force it! Above all, always try hard to follow where the play is leading you. With a good play this won't be too difficult. Indeed, the ability to carry us along with it, and to make skilled actors and actresses from the even the most inexperienced newcomers, is the distinguishing mark of the best theatre. Which is why so many first-class performances of Shakespeare are given by school children. The secret is to put yourself entirely into the playwright's hands, picking up the essential clues to the inner life of the play, the heart of the drama, which he has built into the structure of the play itself. Of course you must learn your lines. Even more important, though, is to learn why you say them.

The cardinal rule is always to take notice of what the playwright is saying and *how he is saying it*. If he's any good at all, the manner of the writing will be tailored to fit the matter he wants to communicate. In the following extract from a modern Christmas play, notice how the scene arranges itself around one particular point. Because of the absurd hilarity of Caspar's speech, and the overpowering atmosphere of veniality and trivialization which it establishes, the sight of Joseph and Mary cuts across the action, bringing everything to a lurching halt, so that Caspar's line, 'What do you want?', is almost forced out of him. If the actor playing Caspar has really let himself go during the long speech, making the best use he can of the material given him by the author, this abrupt change of tone speaks louder than a dozen sermons:

Caspar: (in the role of the 1st innkeeper) We'll have a sixteen-foot high Christmas tree, here by the reception-desk. Flashing lights, plastic fairy on top, with neon-light halo – I mean wand; icicles on the chandeliers; polystyrene snow on the window ledges, aerosol frost on the glass. O, ye blessed Inspector of Taxes! Oh my wonderful bank balance! Personalized Xmas cards in every room, with seasonal greetings from the management and a bar in the Honeymoon Penthouse! Package tours for old-age pensioners, with turkey, plum pudding and a bottle of Spanish plonk! Pop goes the weasel! Tweet goes the robin! Clunk goes the credit card machine! Christmas is coming, the goose is getting fat . . .

Balthasar: (as 2nd innkeeper) Please put a penny in the old man's hat. He hasn't got a credit card.

(Enter Joseph and Mary)

Caspar: (catching sight of Joseph) What do you want? The tradesmen's entrance is round the back!

Joseph: Just a room for my wife and me for the night.

Caspar: Sorry sir. Not a room, not a hole, not a corner. Quite booked up, I'm afraid. On account of the taxation festivities. . .

(from Philip Turner, *How Many Miles to Bethlehem?)*

When you are involved in the job of putting on someone else's play, you must be sure to study the shape of the play as a whole, and also the form and intention of each scene, paying close attention to how these things affect speech, pace, style and variety of playing; finding out where the pauses come, where a particular section of the scene ends and a new section begins, involving perhaps an important change of pace or of the 'tone' of the performance, determining which point in each scene is that scene's particular climax. It's essential to do these things, because playwrights speak through the structure of their plays, the actual way they put things together. As we talk to one another in ordinary conversation, choosing our words and grammatical constructions with a care that is no less scrupulous for having become largely habitual, so the playwright arranges his or her effects. If we want to deliver the message in the way that it is intended, we have to pay attention to the methods employed in order to get it across. I shall have more to say about this in the next chapter.

3. *Making our own plays from other people's (non-theatrical) material*

This includes all those plays, long or short, which individuals or groups of people in a church congregation put together in order to present biblical material, either as a way of underlining a special contemporary relevance or anchoring it in people's own experience, making it 'live' for them by involving them in a drama which includes both themselves and the people in the play. The characters presented may be biblical or drawn from other historical sources, or they may represent the personal testimony of those taking part, or be entirely fictional; the play may be a vignette serving as a 'visual aid' for a sermon, or a three-act drama based upon the life and death of a saint. It may be acted throughout, or partly acted, partly narrated; it may be danced or sung. Because it didn't start out as a play, but as a narrative, a poem or a prayer, our creative work will be centred upon two main objects. First of all we have to find some way of *expanding* the material at hand in order to draw attention to what we understand to be its universal significance or its symbolic meaning for us and all mankind. This isn't as difficult as it sounds, so long as we go about it in the right way. We do it by using examples of the same kind of idea drawn from our own or other people's lives. They have to be the right kind of examples, however – ones chosen because of their emotional and spiritual resonance for us rather than because of the neat way in which they represent the proposition we have in mind. The material we supply in order to expand what is already there in the text must be genuinely our own, and have been felt out, even prayed out, rather than just thought out. If we aren't willing to take this trouble and are content to fall back on any old second-hand material which seems appropriate we shall find our other object almost impossible to achieve. This is the problem of *dialogue.* Although some of the biblical passages we might want to expand contain dialogue, a great many don't. Dialogue which is added on to a narrative remains just that: something added on, which doesn't really belong, and consequently tends to get in the way. In the case of a story taken from the Bible this can be quite upsetting, because biblical narratives set a very high standard of authenticity! The dialogue we want only emerges from a genuine experience of the kind of situation involved.

Brian Clark gives an example of a play based on the description of Christ's nativity, in which the dialogue grew out of a kind of controlled extemporization. The following is a very short extract taken from the longer excerpt included in his book *Group Theatre:*

Chorus: And it came to pass in those days that there went out a decree from Caesar Augustus that all the world should be taxed. And all went to be taxed, everyone into his own city. And Joseph also went up from Galilee, out of the city of David, which is called Bethlehem.

SCENE: BETHLEHEM
Soldier 1: Move along there!
Soldier 2: Get in line! Come on! Move!
Official: Twenty pounds.
Old Man: That's too much.
Official: Twenty pounds, I said. Next!

SCENE: REFUGEES
Soldier 1: Achtung! Achtung!
Soldier 2: In der Reihe! Schweinhund!
Official: Schnell! Dokumente. (Man hands him papers)
   Juden. Namen?
Mary: Maria.
Joseph: Joseph.
Official: Juden.

(Brian Clark, Group Theatre, Pitman 1971, p. 60)

The action then moves swiftly on to a slave auction, before returning to Bethlehem for the 'No Room at the Inn' sequence. Brian Clark comments as follows: 'When we improvized the scenes they were all much longer. Having got the point from them we cut them to the bone, *but the actors were able to be convincing in the short scenes because they were parts of a much larger experience that they had felt*.' (My italics.) Certainly, the actors hadn't themselves been Jewish refugees or human lots in an American slave market; but these things struck a chord in them, and in the audience too, which the original story couldn't do. Perhaps it did the first time they heard it, but repetition dulls the edge of even the most moving scene. The sufferings of the Jews in Nazi Germany, and the terrible indignity of human beings bought and sold as commodities, with all their overtones of similar things which happen today, things we see on television news programmes and read about in the papers are, for us, somehow 'nearer the bone'. We are jolted back into the reality of the actual experience behind the familiar gospel story. As a way of teaching us about the human reality of stories we tend to take for granted and so sharpening the edge of our perception of spiritual truth, drama is unsurpassed.

The provision of realistic dialogue and the need to expand the material by drawing on experiences or incidents in our own or other people's lives are important concerns if we want to produce a recognizable kind of *play*. However, neither is essential for using drama as a way of exploring and exposing the meaning of a biblical text. This can be done much more simply and directly. Some clergy have made extensive use of dramatic techniques in order to convey the real meaning of Christian commitment to young people who are preparing to undertake adult responsibilities as full members of the church. Ivor Moody has sent me a very vivid description of one example of drama being used to bring home what it really means to take the gospel personally and allow it to work at a deep level within the human soul. No words were used in this experiment, and the actors kept precisely to the text without additions of any kind. This really is drama employed in the service of Christ for the deepening of the spiritual life. The occasion was a 'youth camp' arranged by the Fellowship of Catholic Priests for teenagers:

Each day there was a mass in the parish church with a theme for the day. One day we had a healing mass. In my workshop prior to this mass I chose for study a healing miracle of Jesus, in this case the ten lepers. We discussed this miracle and the children quickly grasped the significance of saying 'thank you' to God for what he does for us. Having established the importance of thanksgiving in prayer, we explored a little how important it was for *Jesus* to say 'thank you' to his Heavenly Father – e.g. for food and drink (five loaves and two fishes), for 'revealing all these things not to the wise but babes', and so on. Finally I encouraged all the children in that particular group to portray dramatically the story of the ten lepers. They performed it immediately after the reading of the gospel of the day. 'Jesus' stood in front of the altar silently with head bowed, and the rest of the group took up positions some way down the nave. Each had been 'given' a disability – a limp, disfigured arms, etc. (During the reading of the story) the children began their approach towards Jesus, each acting out his or her disability. Slowly and painfully they reach the feet of Jesus, who, after a short pause, raises his eyes to heaven, stretching his hands out over the assembled company. As he does so, each child begins very slowly to 'unfold' his or her handicap. . . they examine each other in wonderment, and in joy turn their backs on Jesus and run down the aisle skipping and jumping. One suddenly stops, turns and returns to Jesus's feet. He pauses, and then lies flat out on his front, clasping the feet of Jesus, who lowers his gaze from heaven and looks down on the prostrate figure, slowly bringing his arms down to rest upon him.

Father Moody concludes by saying that:

We found the effect on the congregation was stunning and really quite moving. The most profound effect, however, was on the group who performed. . . They discovered they could actually re-create something of the experience of being healed. . .

It must be said that the setting of the eucharist was a crucial factor in the success of Fr Moody's 'experiment'. In these circumstances there is actually no need for specific examples taken from our own and other people's lives. The eucharist has a universal resonance, and includes all experiences of suffering and joy. In such a setting all is deeply and intensely personal. On the other hand, the experience of 'doing the story' instead of just listening to it isn't one which must be confined to a particular structure, either liturgical or ecclesiastical. As we saw in the case of the mystery plays, neither a church service nor a church building are really necessary for religious drama. And in the fact the acting of some biblical narratives may need more space, and more time, than can be provided by the largest church or the longest service. For instance, what could be a better way of re-living the Journey of the Magi than by an actual journey?

This idea had obviously occurred to the educational authorities in the town where I live, because I found myself taking part a few weeks ago in just such a 'happening'. My task was to present myself at the morning assembly at one of our local primary schools in the character of Melchior, and proceed to enlist the help of the children in discovering the birth place of the infant king of the Jews. Having done this (and coped somehow with their astonishment), I was to lead them along the road and through the park to the Comprehensive

School on the hill, where we would join up with two other contingents of seekers from two other primary schools, led by Caspar and Balthasar. There, in the school hall, King Herod and his courtiers were waiting to send us all off to Bethlehem, which for the purpose of the exercise was the parish church half a mile away down the other side of the hill. All went according to plan until we reached Bethlehem; in fact it went rather too well, because we got to the birth-place twenty minutes before the arrival of Mary and Jesus. Fortunately, the Wise Men were able to prevent boredom from setting in at this point by gathering everybody into a circle in the church yard, and telling stories of things that had happened to them on their journeyings. (I silently thanked God for my memories of Amahl and the Night Visitors!) Once inside the church, we all, children and Wise Men, presented gifts to a delighted little boy perched on his mother's knee, who simply couldn't believe his luck. It was all rather beautiful, and totally unforgettable.

My heart went out to the Vicar, however, He had been given the unenviable job of speaking a few words of explanation to follow an event which had quite plainly explained itself. Attempting to stress the importance of imagination in ordinary life, he fell victim to the power of the very thing he was describing. Try as he could he wasn't able to persuade the children to see any difference between their 'real' selves and the roles they were now playing. But this was only to be expected. They had walked a mile, climbed up a hill and down again, and stood waiting in a church yard for twenty minutes, all in the character of 'Wise Men, Servants and Followers'; by this time it was their role and they were sticking to it!

4. Our own play, from our own material

To move from the creative effect of contemplating something old and well known to the challenge presented by a journey into the unknown. . . In starting from ourselves, our own ideas and feelings, we put our trust in the transforming effect that shared imagination has on personal experience. In the next chapter I shall be describing how people learn to work together towards a dramatic happening which actually emerges from their own imagination without the help of a ready-made 'story-line'. The main disadvantage of this approach lies in the fact that, in order to present the results of your creative experience in the form of a play fit to be seen by other people, you have to sit down at some stage in the proceedings, and work out exactly what the final story will be. When exactly you decide to do this is very much up to you. Certainly, I've seen some very effective plays produced by groups who simply 'brain-stormed' their way into a viable piece of theatre. Buf if you intend to start off like this, you must have a particular kind of group to work with – one in which each member is aware of his or her own abilities and shortcomings, and of everyone else's as well. So, sooner or later, every group has to start from scratch, either to attain this kind of awareness or to put it to good use once it has been reached. There really are no short cuts when it comes to making your own play out of your own group experience.

However, the process of working towards some kind of dramatic event which is expressive, imaginative and uniquely your own is one not to be missed. What I've been saying up to now in this book emphasizes the value of drama as an experience in itself rather than as a way of carrying out a definite intention to communicate something to other people. Communication certainly takes place, as we have seen. But it isn't actively sought after. Perhaps this is why it has such a powerful effect on all concerned, players and audience alike! From one point of view, in fact, an audience isn't really necessary. For many people the experience of using drama to explore feelings and attitudes provides the key to a completely new way of looking at life in general and themselves in particular. The discovery of your own natural creativity brings with it increased personal confidence, and the fact that this happens within a group setting makes the sharing of your own thoughts and feelings with other people that much easier. At the same time a quality of creative awareness develops within the group which is very much greater than merely the sum of the individual awarenesses it contains. In a real sense, dramatic creativity comes out of a sense of what you might call 'group enjoyment' – the way that people in the group enjoy being together, the games they play, the jokes they crack, the insights they share, the relational electricity flashing this way and that between them. There really isn't any substitute for this. This is what makes a real play.

I've called it a 'process', but a better word would be journey. One way or another, whether you start with your own material or someone else's, play-making involves a group of men and women who have chosen for a time at least to follow the same road to the same objective. Anyone who has ever been in a play will know what an exhausting slog rehearsals are. It's like climbing a hill; you'd like to stop and look back behind you at all the ground you've already covered. 'I know most of Act 2, and I'm almost word-perfect in Act 1' – but you have to keep climbing away in order to reach the summit, when you'll know exactly what you're doing. Fortunately, you never reach this blessed state. If you did, you'd stop concentrating and lose your awareness, and all that climbing would have been a waste of time.

If you're making your own play this experience of journeying starts as soon as the members of the group have introduced themselves to one another, and you all get down to work together. You literally start climbing before you know where you're going. You know that there is an objective – somehow or other you're going to end up with a play – but you've no idea what it'll be like when you get there. (The same is true to some extent about any play, of course. One's first impression of a script is usually nothing at all like the play as it finally happens. What I'm describing here is really an extreme case of something that concerns drama as a whole, drama as a particular kind of human activity. The dramatic thing is always – you never know!) At some point, always more or less an arbitrary one, because there's always more to be done, you decide to finish exploring and start constructing. You've reached the end of this part of the journey, and you're tired but exhilarated by the things that have happened to you on the way. Whatever the final destination may turn out to be, this much at least will always be true!

And of course, the play itself, the play as presented, will be in the shape of a journey – I can't think of a play that isn't. (Yes, even *Waiting for Godot* is a journey. It doesn't arrive, but this is the whole point; it certainly passes through a crisis and develops the impetus to move on.) As we saw, drama presents us with some kind of conflict, a confrontation of wills, events, personalities, whatever; in an actual play the conflict reaches a climax and a situation of intolerable tension ensues presenting characters and audience with a seemingly insoluble problem. Things can't get worse than this! But of course they do; and the way in which they get worse provides the climax of the play. This can be tragic or comic, but it must be cataclysmic. It must also be *unexpected*; although its connection with the original crisis-situation is very obvious, we somehow couldn't possibly have foreseen it. Something, perhaps, but not this!

Because of the radical nature of this event, a totally new situation exists once it has taken place. In the wake of catastrophe elements within the original situation have now been re-arranged. In the calm which follows the storm the original problem is no longer the same, and a kind of peace can be declared between the opposing forces, signifying the end of the journey.

Put like this, it all sounds very serious, or even portentous. That, however, is a matter of scale. Inside the play, in the subjective world of the characters, everything is just as important as this – either importantly comic or importantly tragic – but the subject-matter of the drama, the play people see from the outside, can be anything at all we want it to be. It can be a glimpse into the deepest reaches of the human soul or a storm in a teacup. (The best example of this basic dramatic scenario that I know actually centres round a storm, albeit an extremely serious one. This is the account of Jonah's relationship with God in the Old Testament. If you read from the beginning as far as Chapter 3, verse 5, where the episode ends, you'll see what I mean. You could do worse than take Jonah as a model when you're designing your own play.) You may be tempted to ask if a play made up by yourselves could ever be as good as one written by a professional, or even a talented amateur. The answer is yes, it could be. In fact, because it will have that special 'ring of truth' which characterizes first-hand experience, it may well be better! And even if it doesn't quite work out the way you'd hoped, and you don't think you could ever manage to get what you really wanted across to the audience, or you're not quite sure what you *do* really want, then remember that the part they're supposed to see isn't your whole experience of drama by any means: it isn't all that *you* have got out of the experiment, either individually or as a group. So you can never completely fail! Even if you have to give the thing up and turn to someone else's ideas for inspiration, you're bound to have learned a lot and benefited from the experience.

The thing is, you see, you can't manufacture creativity. You can't just set out to be creative as a kind of group project. If you're lucky, creativity creeps up on you unawares, usually when you're working hard at something else. What you've just done or said *turns out* to be creative; the joy is in the surprise. You thought you were just messing about, wasting time, doing something dull and obvious, and suddenly . . . So it's always worth a try. What you think is failure may turn out to have been something quite different.

One type of 'home-made' drama which various congregations are experimenting with nowadays is the 'dialogue sermon'. This involves two people who write and perform the script together, so that the authorship is genuinely shared and expresses two quite distinct points of view. The method has frequently been used for teaching purposes of a straightforward kind in which people try to score debating points against each other, arguing either against or in favour of a particular proposition, such as 'religion has been finally disproved by Darwin (or Freud, or Marx)'. You have to be scrupulous about the way you do it if you're aiming at genuine dialogue, however. It can be very tempting to set up a 'straw' opponent and then proceed to demolish him in the cause of theological truth and your own convictions. However, the method can also be used as a way of exploring personal relationships. For example, a husband and wife may celebrate their wedding anniversary within a church setting by writing a dialogue together in which each describes to the other (and to us) exactly what marriage is like from their own point of view. A parent can discuss the problems of growing up with one of his or her children, or two colleagues might explore the experience of working closely alongside someone else. The success of the enterprise, and its effectiveness as drama, will depend on the honesty of the self-disclosure of each to other, and the degree of willingness of each party to take the audience into his or her confidence. It's a fascinating idea, and one which lends itself to all sorts of imaginative variations. But it's no good one of the partners writing the script for both of them to perform so that the message is loaded in one particular direction. Certainly, that could be dramatic enough – but not the kind of group drama we've been thinking about in this chapter!

Notes

The address of Riding Lights is 39 Micklegate, York, YO1 TH; Theatre Roundabout Ltd is at 859 Finchley Road, London NW11 8LX.

Philip Turner's play has not been published, but copies can be obtained from RADIUS (address given in Notes to previous chapter).

It should perhaps be pointed out that one of the most dramatically expressive ways in which a group 'makes use of its own material' is in liturgical dance. Although I have been greatly impressed – and frequently deeply moved – by examples I've seen of this, I don't feel qualified to say anything about it here.

Reference should be made to Martin Blogg, *Time to Dance*, Collins 1984, J. G. Davies, *Liturgical Dance*, SCM Press 1984 and, particularly, G. and J. Stevenson, *Steps of Faith*, Kingsway 1984.

3 The Living Group

Almost anyone can act. By which I mean we're doing it all the time, only we don't notice it. We play different roles according to the things we're doing and the people we're with. This kind of role playing is entirely legitimate. You may be an extremely mild and gentle person, but you're looking for a nervous breakdown if you allow yourself to appear as such when you're faced with the task of bringing a playground full of school-children to order. On the other hand, if your job as a teacher involves counselling you're not going to get many clients if you present yourself as a Company Sergeant-Major. This is all obvious enough. The point I'm making is that we carry out these adjustments in the way we present ourselves automatically. Our sensitivity to the demands of a situation, our ability to pick up clues from people and the facility with which we move into the right gear in order to communicate efficiently with them, these things are second- and third, fourth, and fifth- nature to us.

It's this 'legit' kind of role-playing that you use in drama. If you're parent and child, expert and novice, lover and rival, leader and follower, all at once (or at least in very close sequence) in life, you can be any or all of these things in a play: just so long as you aren't ashamed of your natural facility in taking on roles and try to behave as though it isn't there, or regard it as unworthy or 'neurotic'. If you do, you'll never make an actor (which is why I said 'almost'!). You'll also be kidding yourself: the inability to recognize what you're doing when you change from one role to another is much more neurotic than the simple acceptance that you are naturally and inevitably not one but a whole range of characters.

Children seem to be better at accepting this fact than adults. This is almost certainly because we encourage them to try all sorts of experiments with various roles and call it 'just playing' which, as everybody knows, is a vital part of learning. Adults, on the other hand, are assumed to have learned everything, including how to be people, and so have no need – no excuse – to play like this. This is a pity, because if you watch children playing you can see how they explore the universe in ways that we seem to have forgotten about, creating their own forms of expression as they respond to the prompting of their imagination, endlessly 'trying life out for size':

> Personal play is obvious drama; the whole person or self is used. It is typified by movement and characterization, and we note the dance entering and the experience of being things or people. In personal play, the child journeys about, and takes upon himself the responsibility of playing a role. (Peter Slade, *An Introduction to Child Drama*, p.3.)

Over the years this kind of playing becomes less and less private, more and more a social activity. By the time they are five or six years old, children have started to use a definite plot and to improvize dialogue to fit it; they have reached the stage of testing out various roles as these are suggested, or demanded, by particular kinds of social situation. ('Dramatic play develops from purely egocentric activity to an exercise in co-operation' – Nellie McCaslin, *Creative Dramatics in the Classroom*.)

Practice in playing roles is vital, not only for children but for people of any age. This is an aspect of personality which is, or should be, always open for development. Role itself may be defined as the unit of culture; whenever people meet they take on a particular role with regard to one another. In fact, however, what actually happens is that they share the business of adopting roles among themselves by bestowing and receiving them at the same time according to the process which social psychologists call 'symbolic interactionism', a complex procedure in which you're likely to find yourself accepting a particular role that you don't want and the other person doesn't really intend you to have; you just think they do! At some point it seems that our ability to pick up the right clues about how people *really* see us, what they really expect or want from us, begins to break down. We get set in a role – or a range of roles – and we stop experimenting. The trouble is, they may not be appropriate roles. In fact some of them are almost bound to be inappropriate. People change, and they don't all change at once or in the same direction. If you want to love and understand them, and be loved and understood by them, you've got to keep on your toes! The need for personal development, which means skill and sensitivity in personal *relationships,* continues as long as life lasts; and drama is a way of helping people to develop because it helps them to *explore.*

Once they can get over their shyness, that is. Grown men and women don't like the idea of playing games like kids. Even if they can see the point in pretending to be someone else in order to experience the kind of thing someone else might feel, the exercise makes them self-conscious. It's bound to, of course; if the 'self' you've got is very important to you and you find it very useful and have spent a long time perfecting it – if it's a policeman's, or a business executive's, or a vicar's self – then you'll feel a bit naked without it and tend to cling to it as much as you possibly can. If your sense of self is already threatened and reduced by the situation you find yourself in, as in the case with the patients with whom I work in dramatherapy sessions, then you certainly don't want to play games that are childish and silly. ('It's bad enough being here at all without being made fools of . . .') Some of the games that leaders of drama groups, whether therapeutic, educational or merely recreational, think up for their members can seem, at first sight, to be a bit inane. Children wouldn't think them so, because children, like adults at parties, are usually game for almost anything, and specially a game; but sensible, serious adult folk need to be reassured about the serious purpose of everything that they are seen to do in public. Most of these games and exercises are quite skilfully designed to solve the problems of shyness and 'dignity' that they appear at first to be creating. They are intended to make us more aware of one another and heightened self-consciousness is an inevitable stage that we have to pass through on the way. Once you realize that other people feel the way you do by abandoning your own natural defensiveness long enough to have a really good look at them, the problem of joining in with what they're doing, even though it may seem a strange way of learning how to act – either in plays or in life – is largely resolved. You don't mind playing games with people you *know,* do you? You feel safe with people you know.

This is a rather sketchy description of a process of helping people to relax in one another's company which has been treated in much greater depth elsewhere (see, for example, the books by Donna Brandis and Howard Phillips, and Dorothy and Gordon Langley, mentioned at the end of this chapter). I can only say that facile as it may seem, in my own experience it always works, if I myself am willing to work at it.

Playing and safety go together: if you feel safe, you're willing to allow yourself to play. I have no doubt at all that this kind of experimental role-playing is a natural human function. It is certainly the foundation of drama. Every kind of theatre, from a mimed nativity play to Shakespeare's *King Lear,* is based on it. Theatre begins in security and leads on to adventure. The child who plays so happily by himself when he (or she) thinks no one is paying attention begins to share his games with his friends, and to play games which can't be played satisfactorily *without* them. The crucial step is taken when these games are eventually allowed to become really public: when they begin to be designed in order to be shown to other people. This is a big step – particularly for adults – but it is one which proceeds from, and in a real sense depends on, the original impulse and can't be properly understood in isolation from it.

The best way to make your own theatrical presentation, if this is your aim, is to start from drama in its basic form, the exploration of personal roles and inter-personal situations. As I said, the two things go together and can't be separated. Theatre starts from drama, and drama starts from scratch. In other words, it starts from getting used to people and building up an atmosphere of confidence within the group. This is something that a lot of amateur play-makers seem to forget. And not only amateurs either! Perhaps it's so obvious that people overlook it!

Or perhaps it's neglected because it can be a bit embarrassing at first. Real emotion isn't always easy to acknowledge either in yourself or in other people. Drama, however, is all about emotion, and it can't be avoided. Feeling emotion, expressing it, and finally portraying it. Portraying it from the inside, where it originates. Whatever you intend to create in the way of theatre, whatever kind of play you have in mind, emotion will be your raw material. So it's no use feeling embarrassed when you find yourself getting too excited, or too 'silly', or too upset by the feelings that are beginning to emerge within the group. Drama involves experiment and discovery within a particular area of human experience, that of the relationship between our personal life and our social role, and the drama games which we use in order to explore this area are aimed precisely at developing an awareness of how emotions are transmitted between, shared among, and intimately involved with, *other people.* A group that has really got to know itself in this way, whose members have learned to trust one another, which means trust themselves *to* one another – will certainly find that the effort pays off when it comes to presenting a play to other people. After all, you don't ever know how others are going to react, do you? So it definitely helps if you do know what to expect from yourselves. You might say that it's the group that provides the courage to produce good theatre from raw drama. The idea of the play may be someone else's, but its life is cradled in the emotions and insights of the people who act in it.

As we saw in the last chapter, there are many different kinds of religious theatre, many different uses to which drama can be put in order to communicate the quality of Christian experience. Some of these involve using plays or sketches or musical shows which arrive in a ready-to-be-presented state, having been written and put together by someone else and produced once or even many times before. Others are genuinely home-grown and had no prior existence apart from the experience and imagination of the group that created them. Experience in basic drama, 'group-building', is important for both kinds of theatre. I've included a few exercises here in order to give some idea of the kind of thing I mean. As you can see, they cover several sessions.

1. Things to do in order to build general confidence and group cohesion

(At the beginning of rehearsals these may take up an entire session. When you start working on the play itself, it's a good idea to 'warm up' by doing a few of these exercises as an introduction to each session.)

(*a*) Try out ways of sharing experiences of an emotional kind, starting with comparatively 'safe' methods and gradually becoming more adventurous. Suggestions:

(i) Members of the group write the names of various emotions on pieces of card. These are then shuffled, and a card taken out at random (e.g. Fear). This card is passed round the group from hand to hand, each member saying what kind of situation or idea makes him or her particularly afraid. Continue with the rest of the cards. End by discussing feelings and how to come to terms with them.

(ii) Working in pairs, one member of each pair puts his or her partner into a pose which expresses a particular emotion (e.g. Joy, Sorrow). These poses are considered and discussed by the group. How expressive are they? What do they remind us of? The other partner now becomes the 'sculptor' and fashions his or her partner to represent a contrasting emotion, which is then discussed.

(iii) This can be extended by dividing the main group into smaller ones, each of which decides on its own 'dramatic situation' (e.g. lost children, house on fire, family holiday, etc.). Each group is given three emotions to portray (e.g. Anxiety, Panic, Relief, or Sorrow, Bitterness, Acceptance), and performs a short mimed play which moves from the first emotion to the third by way of the second. Both the emotions and the plots are guessed by the other groups. Discussion.

(*b*) Try out ways of taking on someone else's feeling or experience as if it were yours.

(i) Members tell their partners about something that has happened to them during the previous week which has affected them personally. Having done this, they give their neighbour permission to tell the whole group. (Obviously, if the incident was too painful, they won't mention it; but it often turns out that it's easier to have someone say things on your behalf than to tell the whole group yourself.) After everyone has been given the opportunity to take part, the same procedure can be used for the vicarious disclosure of emotions or attitudes.

(ii) Each member of the group selects an object in the room (a book, a cushion, a potted plant, a fire-bucket, anything at all). Trying to imagine the 'experiences' of the object as if it were sensate, they speak in character: 'I've been standing here in the corner by the door for five years. I'm never bored, because it's my nature to stand by doors. I used to be green, but last year a girl on a Youth Opportunities Programme painted me red. Oh, I wish there was a fire! It would be my finest hour!' etc.

(iii) Members of the group make choices and arrangements *as if they were* their partners in the group. This starts at the simple level of guessing what your partner's tastes are in food, clothes, music etc.: 'If I invited you to dinner, I'd prepare a menu like this. . . If I were buying you an outfit you'd really like I'd start with. . .' Working in threes, one member asks another questions about him/herself which the third person answers on his/her behalf, as if they themselves actually were the one being questioned. Group members act scenes 'being' one another in a restaurant, a dress shop, a record or book shop. A good way to finish is by setting up a fashion parade in which group members can appear first of all in their partner's persona, pretending to wear the outfit they chose for him or her, and then as themselves, in the partner's choice for them. You need a 'presenter' for this, who describes the outfits and introduces the models. (It's great fun!)

(iv) As group identity increases, members should be encouraged to take on responsibility for expressing thoughts and feelings on behalf of one another. One way you can do this is by simply saying something like, 'I think Angela's feeling upset today. Perhaps she feels etc. . .' A more direct way would be to put your hand on Angela's arm and speak as if you were her. It would be confusing (and undramatic!) if you simply went straight ahead and did this, so you signal your intention by introducing yourself in your new role: 'I'm Angela, and I want to tell you that you're all getting on my nerves! You know I've got a headache, and you know why, because I told you, and you're playing the noisiest games you can think of!' You can stand alongside Angela to do this, or just behind her, with your hands on her shoulders as if you were presenting her to the group. Your diagnosis won't always be right, but Angela will usually be grateful that someone has made the effort to see things from her point of view.

(*c*) From time to time it's a good idea to 'take the group's temperature'; that is, try to assess how people are beginning to relate to one another, the nature of the various undercurrents of opinion and attitude within the group, the alliances that form and re-form, the 'pecking-order' among its members. Is it a group at all, or simply a number of separate individuals whose attitude to one another is one of rivalry, not co-operation? (It shouldn't be, by now!) When one person asks to be left out of whatever the group is doing at the time, how do people react? How do they react to other members who feel impelled to give support to the non-participant and seem to be 'splitting the group'? Do you ever make one another *laugh?* Again, all this can be discussed, and if you're a specialist in group dynamics, you can have a go at analysing the various social processes at work! However, the thing that matters most is the over-all cohesion of the group, its sense of being a unity within itself. The best way of assessing this is not verbal at all, and takes much less time than a full-blown discussion. Like Section (*b*)(iv) above, it's a technique borrowed from psychodrama, where it is usually called 'sculpting'. What you do is to get various members of the group (chosen at random, or better still, volunteers) to arrange the whole group as a kind of three-dimensional tableau or corporate statue, according to the particular relationships which they distinguish within the group. In this way each 'sculptor' can demonstrate how he or she 'sees' the group and also how he or she feels the group 'sees' *itself*. No verbal description is half so effective as 'sculpting'. It's very easy to do, once you've got the idea, and gives immediate insight, a kind of 3D instant snap-shot of the state of affairs which exists at a particular juncture in the group's life as this is experienced by a particular person in the group. It's a moving picture (in more than one sense of the word!) because various members re-arrange it according to their own perceptions, and people who have been placed in various attitudes and positions adjust themselves according to the way they feel they *should* have been placed, the impression that they really intend to give about themselves – which may be quite different from the one they are actually giving. This exercise often leads into discussion and should of course be allowed to do so if people want to talk about what it has revealed to them. Sometimes, however, it's enough to let it speak for itself, and move on from there.

2. Working towards the play

(This is a play you've already got, rather than one you're trying to make for yourselves. That comes in the next section.)

Once you feel yourselves to be a group as well as a collection of individuals you're in a position to begin thinking about the play in a systematic and purposeful way, with a certain degree of assurance that something worthwhile will eventually emerge. Not everything you do will be of high artistic merit, but it will be something real because your group is real. You're frank and free and confident in one another's regard and affection, and you're both adventurous and secure. In a word, your group is a proper medium for communicating truth. You may of course think that all Christian groups are like this to begin with, without having to work at it. After all, it's what Christianity is all about, isn't it? The answer to that is, Yes it is, and No, they're not! All the same, Christian drama groups do start off with a very considerable advantage. They can pray together and worship alongside one another. They share the same scriptural tradition and can comfort one another with the same assurance of Christian hope. At the deepest and most profound level they are indissolubly joined together within and through Christ, co-heirs to the promise that he embodies, members of him and one another. As they set about the task of proclaiming truth and love by means of drama and story they are reassured that it's a method Jesus himself favoured.

All the same, the kind of mutual acceptance and understanding you need both for drama and for life isn't easy to achieve. I believe that without God's help you can't achieve it at all. Even with his help, as St Paul knew so very well, you have to work at it. The place of prayer in Christian play-making should have been mentioned in the first section, as the first thing to do to 'build confidence and group cohesion'. Never mind, I'm mentioning it now. It's always very important indeed, and can be crucial. I remember working once with a highly professional Christian theatre group who were short of an actor and borrowed me for one of their plays. We were going to have to present it after only a single day's full rehearsal, which barely gave us time to learn our lines. Nobody would choose to work in such circumstances, of course, but there wasn't any choice. The company either made the best of a bad job and went ahead, or excused themselves from performing and disappointed the audience which had been looking forward so much to their visit. I wasn't looking forward to the show at all, and I wasn't the only one, either! This was a surprising company, however. Every time we came to a problem either of interpretation or staging – or forgetting lines – the actors put their arms round one another and offered the situation to God. They didn't do this in any pietistic way, as a kind of excuse for their own lack of courage, but confidently and enthusiastically invoked the Holy Spirit to provide the fuel necessary to get the machinery going again, and the show on the road. And that's what happened.

However, this is a digression, even though an important one, perhaps. What I want to concentrate on here is – the importance of *concentration*. It goes without saying that an actor must attend very strictly to what he's doing in the performance itself; what isn't so obvious is the degree of concentration on the play which is necessary before you begin acting in it, even before you start to learn the lines.

I used to think that people were put off Shakespeare's plays by having to study them at school. The great joy of plays is doing them, not reading them – and particularly not pulling them to pieces and studying them under some kind of literary microscope. When you actually take part in a play by Shakespeare, either as an actor or a member of the audience, and the chrysalis of archaic words and obscure old-fashioned ideas splits open to liberate the quivering, pulsing, resplendent creature within, you feel you never want to go back to the text again. These are plays, after all! Let's enjoy them for what they really are.

Unfortunately, though, if you want to release all this beauty, all this life, which sleeps in any good play, you can't simply hurl yourself at it. The uniqueness of the play which is its living essence, emerges from a combination of two different kinds of understanding, the creative and the interpretative. These are both varieties of imagination, but they work in different ways. The insight and sensitivity of actors and producer are like a surgeon's scalpel which is used to explore the playwright's original conception. I say a surgeon rather than a midwife, which is the more obvious metaphor to use, because I want to emphasize the very precise skill and the intimate knowledge of the nature of the individual organism necessary in order to carry out the operation. Any actor or producer can impose his or her own intentions upon the suffering playwright; but to allow the play itself to speak as it should – that is, through the *joint efforts* of both author and presenters – requires a good deal of hard work and self-discipline. 'One of the privileges of doing works from the past', says Jonathan Miller, 'is to break bread with the dead.' I might add at this point that the plays which delighted me the most when I came eventually to act in them were the same dull texts I'd had to dissect so many years ago in Eng. Lit.!

Brian Clark has put this very well indeed: 'I cannot emphasize too strongly the importance of not breaking the cohesion of a play' (in order, that is, to "get inside it") 'before it has been thoroughly understood *in its own terms*. We must not seek for relevances and reverberations before we hear the initial message. Spend as much time and effort as you can to ensure that this part of the exploration is thoroughly done.' He goes on to say: 'If the play is from a past time make sure you understand the references. Do not take it for granted that words have the same meaning today.' This is very important indeed for religious theatre. If the material belongs to another age, we want to 'make it relevant for today's audience'. But we must be sure we understand it before we begin to re-interpret it in the light of our own contemporary experience. A text needs thinking about, praying about, even dreaming about, before we are ready to enter into partnership with it. *'Contemplation'* is the word that springs to mind: whereas nobody would claim that a play should be an object of worship, it is certainly a fit subject for contemplation. Only this way will it yield all it contains for us. All this is summed up in Brian Clark's injunction upon all who work with plays written by someone else to 'stay with the text'. When you approach such a play you come up against a whole world of experience, social, cultural, psychological and spiritual which may or may not be like yours, but never, ever, *is* yours. This background of someone else's thinking and experience is the play's essential setting, and it affects the nature of the play itself. 'It's all there in the text; all I did was look. You *have* to *look,* you know.' This was the reply I got from Walter Hudd when I commented on the depth and subtlety of his performance as the French king in *Henry V.* I was only a beginner at the time, fresh out of drama school, but I've never forgotten what he said, because it seemed so surprising. I'd never come across a text-oriented actor before, and had always concentrated on finding things in my own experience which I could use the play to develop and explore. What I didn't fully understand until 'Dickie' Hudd pointed it out to me, was that it's a two-way relationship. If you can 'un-lock' a play, the play will 'un-lock' you.

Sometimes the material you have to get to know is particularly difficult to accommodate for reasons of style. I can think of two kinds of play in which this is very much the case; those written in old-fashioned or highly poeticized language, and those which use material not originally intended for acting – documentaries and plays, derived from narrative passages in books (the Bible, for instance). William Fry, writing in RADIUS Magazine, gives an example of the best way of dealing with Shakespeare 'from the inside':

Take this passage from *Hamlet,* Act II Scene 2. 'Gentlemen, you are welcome to Elsinore. Your hands, come: the appurtenance of welcome is fashion and ceremony: let me comply with you in this garb, lest my extent to the players, which I tell you, must show fairly, outwards, should appear more like entertainment than yours.' Rudely translated, this might read: 'Well, friends, it's nice to see you. Shake hands, come on: I'm sure you don't want a lot of fuss and formality: I'm greeting you like this, so that you won't think I'm being nicer to the actors (you see I have to be very polite to them) and giving them a better time than you.'

Sometimes you have to overcome a considerable stylistic barrier in order to separate what the text is actually saying from the way in which it is saying it. However, you can't simply leap over the barrier and substitute your own words for what the playwright wrote, because the original style is very important. It's at least half of the message you must convey, so that when you've discovered exactly what the passage means you have then to work out why it has been put the way it has, and share this with the audience, too. (For example, in the passage quoted above, all sorts of information about Hamlet's convoluted way of organizing his own thoughts, his ambivalent attitude towards people who show him friendship or love, his difficulty in acting spontaneously without thinking everything out and justifying it to himself first, as well as Shakespeare's own delight in presenting the etiquette of seventeenth-century court life to be savoured by his audience, has to be included in the final communication. As you can see, there's a lot of work to be done!) I can vouch for the effectiveness of this approach so long as it is combined with the effort to discover the physical patterns which express our intellectual understanding; but these can only emerge from the kind of exploration of group experience which I described earlier on. When the two come together, marvellous things can happen. One of the most remarkable experiences of my own life as an actor was as a member of the group which took Joan Littlewood's production of *Macbeth* to Moscow in 1958, when we used an approach like the one described by William Fry to take the text to pieces and put it back again in order to get to the heart of the play.

Another production I shall never forget, but one which I wasn't fortunate enough to take part in myself, except as a member of the audience, was Peter Cheeseman's documentary about the Primitive Methodist Church, *The Burning Mountain*. I say Peter Cheeseman's production; in fact this play was entirely constructed by the company, using material from contemporary sources. In other words, there was no actual written text for a play – no dialogue, no stage directions, no ready-made list of characters or description of settings. Everything that happened during the performance had evolved from the performers' devoted study of whatever they could find about nineteenth-century Stoke which had any bearing on the life and death of the two founders of the movement, Hugh Bourne and William Clowes. The work of the Victoria Theatre, Stoke-on-Trent, is the best example I know of a genuine 'group theatre' – one where the business of making relationships and the intention to make a play which embodies and presents these relationships in the form of a work of dramatic art comes together with amazing results to produce an experience in which all present, actors and audience alike, find themselves deeply involved at the most personal level. I used the word 'devoted' to describe the actors' state of mind and heart. From one point of view this is misleading, as I'm reasonably sure that none of the people who 'made' the play was actually a practising Christian. Certainly there were no Primitive Methodists among them. I had recently left the company myself, in order to return to the whole-time ministry, and I was dumbfounded by what I saw. I'd no idea that my former friends in the cast had so much religious feeling in them. What I saw here was true, it was *real*. I wasn't the only person either among the audience or in the arena itself who was in tears that night. The question as to where it had come from I leave you to consider (it certainly wasn't from me!). But I know what it was that had brought it out of them. It was the discipline involved in surrendering to the material they were working on that had allowed the quality of Bourne's and Clowes' original experience to emerge. This was a religious play constructed and performed by a group of non-Christians. We have to remember of course that the Stoke company are extremely talented and very highly skilled. Even so, the fact remains that a Christian congregation, using material of an explicitly sacred kind – one of the gospel narratives, for instance – starts off with a considerable advantage when it comes to communicating religious truth in play form, so long as it sticks to certain basic rules which hold good for any kind of theatre: the principle of group cohesion and solidarity, that of mutual trust and acceptance, and the basic attitude of mind according to which the actors and producer immerse themselves as deeply as they can in the material to be presented.

I have called this the principle of contemplation. The idea of using this word to describe a secular activity such as play-making was suggested to me by Peter Dodson, an Anglican priest who is well-known for having discovered a quite remarkable way of approaching the Bible for the purpose of leading prayer groups in parishes. With his permission, I'd like to describe this here. (I'm going to do this in my own words but I'm very conscious of the fact that he puts it much better in his own book, *Towards Contemplation – A Practical Introduction to Prayer Groups.*) The approach involves an introductory exercise, three stages of contemplative prayer, and a period of discussion and sharing.

Introduction: 'As we sit quietly we allow God to call us into his rest, using words like those from Matthew 11.28 and Psalm 46.10. "Come to me, all whose work is hard, whose load is heavy: and I will give you rest. . ." "Be still and know that I AM God. . ." "Come to me . . . Be still . . . and rest . . . Come . . . rest . . . Come . . . rest." We spend just a couple of minutes, allowing these two "words" to become part of the rhythm of our breathing and of our lives: "Come (as we breathe in) . . . rest (as we breathe out) . . . Come . . . rest . . . Come . . . rest." ' (Silence for two minutes.)

Stage I: Using a passage from the Bible, the leader directs the group towards an intellectual understanding of the text which is to be contemplated: 'Now bring to *mind* the particular "words" we have selected for this contemplative prayer exercise. Let the words come to life in our minds in all their richness. Let the words of God become rooted, incarnate, alive and active in the *thinking* part of our nature.'

Stage II: In this stage, following a period of silence in which the group has tried to make the biblical message 'part of our own mental vocabulary', intellectual understanding is internalized in order to become emotional experience: 'And now, as far as possible, take the Word of God to *heart*. Desire the Word that you may grow by it. Let the Word dwell in you, richly, in all wisdom, love and power. Receive the Word which is able to save. . .'

Stage III: Another period of silence leads to a time when this new depth of perception is turned outwards towards the world so that it may be used for the living out of God's message: 'And now we broaden our vision to include the church family of which we are members . . . we go on using that God-given gift of imagination, achieving a vision of his concern for the life of our nation, the world and the whole of creation.'

This last stage may be developed, says Peter Dodson, into 'a much freer expression of concern for the well-being of others'. Sometimes, he tells me, it can lead to the sharing of deep personal experiences which have been given a new clarity and force during the time of the exercise. Memories, visions, hopes and fears are transformed by concentration on God. Sometimes this new and deeper spiritual perception is expressed in the form of symbols and metaphors that can be communicated to others. For example, the experience of reconciliation to God may express itself in a vivid thought-picture of greeting your own father after many years of separation, perhaps involving feelings of estrangement or even bitterness, and running towards him on a railway-station platform, throwing yourself into his arms, 'Father, I love you!. . .'

I've described all this in order to demonstrate that prayer of this kind can lead into something which is very close to the personal drama which lies at the heart of theatre. There are obvious differences between a drama-session and a prayer-group. However, the idea that prayer is private and drama public is a misleading over-simplification. There *is* an important connection between the two kinds of happening. Both are experiences of relationship intensified to the point of demanding expression in the form of metaphor and symbol. The same kind of spontaneous 'imaging forth' which occurs in Peter Dodson's groups may also happen when Christians have the task of discovering the inner personal meaning of a passage from the Bible and sharing it with an audience in the form of a play. The 'word' need not necessarily be one of God's direct statements delivered by Jesus, or by one of the prophets or evangelists. It can just as well be an indirect communication, a parable or a biblical narrative expressing God's saving purpose towards mankind. The intention of drama is to bring home to us the living relevance of the truth about persons to help us really *know* what we only think we know, or only know *about*. If we want to illustrate a well-known story like the narrative of Jesus's birth or the events surrounding his passion and resurrection with similar situations which might occur today, or have occurred in recent history, we must do it from the inside, rather than the outside. Otherwise, our attempt to achieve 'relevance' will only appear artificial and rather cheap, as if we've

DRAMA

Self-contained – created – structured interaction between individuals within environment. (Symbolism unconscious and shared only by participants.)

THEATRE

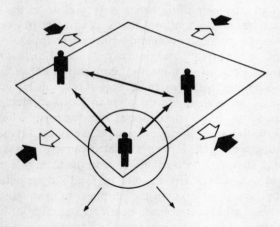

The barrier is broken and the total structure is directed outwards. At the same time the individual interacts with the audience, and vice-versa. (Dramatic symbol organized for communication to others.)

(Diagrams by Roland Metcalfe, used by permission. For a comprehensive examination of the relationship between drama and theatre, see Lynn McGregor, Maggie Tate and Ken Robinson, *Learning Through Drama*, Heinemann 1977.)

only dragged these things in because we want to be clever and 'with it'. To be genuinely 'with it' we ourselves must actually have experienced the truth of it by an intense and concerted effort of the imagination. We must feel ourselves to be left with no alternative than to share what we ourselves have actually discovered.

3. *Imagining and revealing*

For something to be symbolic – that is, for it to express an 'inner' meaning we can understand and recognize and make part of our conscious lives – it must have *shape*. It's the shape of an event which makes it stand out from other things as being important and significant. If drama is using acting and role play in order to explore the meaning of our personal lives, then *theatre* is the way we organize what we discover in drama into the kind of shape which is able to communicate this meaning to other people. Also, by a kind of reflection, to ourselves (see diagram opposite). You could say theatre is the 'language of drama'. Like all languages, it helps us organize our own thoughts as well as communicating our thinking to others. Although it uses words, it doesn't depend on them: its meaning comes across through events and the order in which they happen. However difficult it may be to recognize the process in some plays, particularly modern ones, theatre always represents a finished happening. It shows how some kind of relationship, or stage within a relationship, begins, develops and ends. The relationship must be dramatic, however, and this means that whether tragic or comic, it must include an element of conflict, for both tragedy and comedy consist in the meeting of feelings and ideas which appear to us at some point in the proceedings to be irreconcilable, for just as symbols represent 'the coincidence of opposites', the triumph of meaning over nonsense, so do plays. For drama to be made into theatre its events and relationships must be consciously organized around the resolution of conflict. You can use the conflicts which exist within a group – once the people in it are confident enough to allow them to appear, that is – in order to develop drama, but the co-operation of the entire group is essential when it comes to building a play around those conflicts, or similar ones suggested by them, and so producing genuine theatre. For a long time now, drama teachers in schools have been making use of the raw material which emerges from improvized scenes and situations in the way of conflicting feelings, attitudes and ideas in order to get children to construct their own plays. The fact that you can express yourself, or certain parts of yourself, so much more freely when you're pretending to be someone else, doesn't apply only to children, of course. Once a group of adults has lost some of its initial self-consciousness, it too can begin to work towards theatre in this way. The advantages of do-it-yourself theatre are tremendous so far as increased self-confidence goes; it's so much easier than you'd imagine if you've never tried it. Even if you decide not to show your play to anyone else, the understanding and experience you gain is of the greatest help when you have to take part in plays written by other people.

I'd like to mention two ways in which a group can begin to move in this direction. The first is a well-tried method taken from educational drama, and involves the choice of an abstract idea which will provide the theme for dramatic exploration. You could use the idea of 'love', or 'hate', 'justice', or 'forgiveness'. The theme may be suggested by the group leader, as often happens in educational drama, or it may be democratically decided upon by the group, the method I myself prefer to use. In the following example, the starting point is the idea of 'creative compromise'.

1. The group pass the idea around among themselves, each member in turn mentioning 'something I won't ever compromise about'. When everyone has contributed, the process is repeated, with everyone describing occasions in their life when they have had to compromise.

2. The group divides into two halves, one of which comes to some conclusions about how the room itself could be improved. Perhaps the furniture could be re-arranged and rostra provided, the walls painted a different colour, a drinks-dispenser installed, etc. In the meantime the other half of the group have been discussing how much they like the room as it is – they're used to it, it has happy memories for them, they have managed to make it 'workable' for drama purposes. The first group tries to convince the second of the need for change and 'improvement'; the second group resists the idea. Some kind of compromise is eventually arrived at.

3. The scene is a street market. Pairs of group-members haggle over prices. After a time they exchange roles, the stallholders becoming the bargain-hunters.

4. Pretending to be architects, pairs set about the task of

designing a bridge together. One argues for aesthetic effect, the other for functional utility. (Building materials must be decided upon, too!)

5.   Groups of three improvize situations in which one has to act as a mediator between conflicting parties in a divorce case, a business disagreement, an international dispute, etc.

This last exercise moves naturally into role-play as the rest of the group are encouraged to take part in the improvized drama which seems to provoke most interest, whichever it may happen to be. At this point, the leader suggests that the group takes the characters and the situation and makes a play out of them. There will have to be some discussion and experiment as to how this can be done with the material at hand, but the essential elements are already there – the characters and the crisis out of which the play can grow.

In this example, both have been suggested by the group leader who 'set up' the situation by deciding what kinds of conflict situation should take place between which kinds of people. There's no need to be as directive as this, of course, particularly with an adult group, and you may find it possible to work on a play in which not only the dialogue, but the plot and the personages involved have all been 'generated' by the cast. It certainly never does to underestimate people's imagination. One of the ways that I like best to work with a group depends almost entirely on the innate skill everyone has for making some kind of immediate sense of the relationship among any group of individuals that is presented to them. In order to do this, I, as group leader, dispense with all suggestions as to what kind of drama I have in mind. In fact, I have no pre-conceived ideas about it at all. I just want to see what emerges when you give the imagination free rein. In order to clear the decks as effectively as possible, I simply take an individual aside and ask him or her to go and take up a position within the acting area – standing, walking about, sitting at a table etc. He or she can be feeling a powerful emotion, or just simply 'being'. There should be no attempt at playing a role or impersonating anyone. Then I go up to another person in the group and ask them to join the first one. They, too, have a choice as to where they will stand or sit, and what, if anything, they should be feeling like. A third person may join in, and so on, although if you're doing this for the first time with a new group it's a good idea to limit the numbers within the acting area to two or three. Then I ask the remaining people present what they think is going on in the scene before them. What is the relationship between these people? What kind of people are they? What has been happening before this? Who, in fact, *are* they?

The surprising thing is that they always tell me. 'One is a bored wife who has been out shopping all day without any appreciable results. The things she wanted were either too expensive or out of stock. That's one reason why she isn't talking to the man standing by the table. He's her husband and they had a row before he went to work this morning. He'd like to make it up; in fact, he's been waiting eagerly to get home in order to tell her how much he loves her. At the moment he can't, because their teenage daughter is doing her homework and it would be embarrassing to bring it all up in front of her. That's her, sitting at the table.' And so on. This is all quite fascinating because I myself didn't know anything at all about this, nor did the 'wife', 'husband', and 'teenage daughter' concerned. But not a word has been said by any of us.

All of which serves to illustrate a basic rule of theatre, which I shall be returning to later on. An audience is intrigued by what they themselves think is happening before them. It doesn't have to be spelled out for them. Present them with a challenge and they are only too eager to rise to it. In this case their eagerness to participate in and enjoy a *play* challenges them to make something real out of almost nothing at all. Audiences enjoy a challenge – it's their way of taking part in the drama. No wonder actors talk in terms of 'letting the audience do the work'! No wonder, either, that the idea of group theatre has taken such a hold of people's imagination during the last twenty or thirty years. In this case, what started as a trick leads almost inevitably into something entirely different, as the group begins to understand its own innate abilities in the way of imagination and creativity. This really is their play, they've all had a hand in getting it going. Now all that's needed is to give it some kind of shape so that it can develop out of a dramatic situation into a piece of real theatre. Now the relationships between the characters are established, the dialogue begins to flow without much difficulty.

First of all, however, the gap that still exists within the group between 'actors' and 'audience' must somehow be bridged. This isn't as difficult as you may suppose. Once people actually start to use their imaginations in this creative way, they lose a good deal of their fear of taking part and becoming 'characters' themselves. I said earlier that the portrayal of character emerges from particular situations. This idea is well expressed by Gavin Bolton in the following description of the way children can work from the representation of individual states of mind and body which aren't their own towards the creation of really expressive symbols, which have a universal meaning, so that an imaginative game becomes the kind of metaphor of human life which is the hall-mark of genuine drama, from Aeschylus to Samuel Beckett:

> 'Let's be pirates, Sir.' In fact, children cannot be pirates: they can only be pirates who have to keep their eyes skinned because danger is round the corner, or pirates who must find the treasure before dark, or pirates who want their fair share of the loot, and so on. . .

He goes on to describe how enthusiasm to pretend leads into actions which set in train experiences possessing a kind of meaning far wider than the original impulse:

①	②	③
Pirates who have to keep their eyes skinned for dangers.	The child may draw on what he knows of anticipating danger or a threat.	The drama may become about people who never feel safe.
Pirates who must find the treasure before dark.	The child may draw on what he knows of being short of time.	The drama may become about people who work to a deadline.
Pirates who want their fair share of the loot.	The child may draw on his experience of sharing and not trusting.	The drama may become about people who distrust each other.

It is at this third stage, as children begin to share a universal experience, that individual imitation becomes a shared dramatic experience.

Even taking into account the fact that it needn't be 'Pirates' – it could be 'Early Christians' or 'Single Parents' – this is obviously much easier for children than adults, who have largely forgotten how to lose themselves in this kind of playing. But the principle remains the same; and even adults can imagine, given the chance. All they need is a little help on re-discovering powers that have often lain dormant for years. Adults can't do this individually because they feel self-conscious; it has to come from group experience. When you really participate, you haven't time to be thinking about 'what other people think of me behaving like this'. It's at this point that all the hard work that has been put in to build the group starts to pay off, as people share their delight in re-discovering something they thought they had lost forever. A group that has made this discovery, and made it *together,* has truly 'come of age'. Now it's ready to begin work!

Notes

Books and articles mentioned in this chapter are:

Gavin M. Bolton, 'Drama as Metaphor', *Young Drama,* 4 February 1976

Donna Brandis & Howard Phillips, *Gamester's Handbook,* Hutchinson 1977

Brian Clark, *Group Theatre,* Pitman 1971

Peter Dodson, *Towards Contemplation,* Fairacres Publications 1977

William Fry, 'Rehearsing Through an Analogue', RADIUS, 11, 44, 1983

Dorothy M. & Gordon E. Langley, *Dramatherapy and Psychiatry,* Croom Helm 1983

Nellie McCaslin, *Creative Dramatics in the Classroom,* Longmans 1982

Peter Slade, *An Introduction to Child Drama,* University of London Press 1958

4   Doing it Yourselves

It must be admitted that putting a play together in the way I've been describing is a bit frightening if you've never done this kind of thing before. It all seems so different from the conventional approach in which you simply rehearse a play someone else has written, doing your best to remember the lines and the moves. This way you have first of all to create your own raw material in the way of ideas, incidents, characters and relationships; then you must write the play yourselves, making use of the things you have discovered (and also those that have discovered you!); then, and only then, can you start learning lines and practising moves. The advantage here, of course, is that the world of your own play, the ideas and feelings it embodies, are yours from the beginning. You haven't had to discover the inner reality of somebody else's vision, and this means that both learning lines and rehearsing particular scenes are easier than for a play that isn't your own in this special sense, but has to be made yours by a concentrated effort of imagination and understanding – the 'contemplation' described in the last chapter.

The main draw-back involved in the do-it-yourself method is the sheer technical difficulty of fashioning a play, a piece of theatre out of the free-flowing dramatic material that your improvization has supplied you with. Somehow, out of all this, a play must be constructed which has a beginning, a middle and an end. The audience mustn't know what's going to happen and they must be surprised when it does happen. Surprised but not incredulous: there must be the sense of inevitability which is the hall-mark of all real theatre. To achieve this effect takes a lot of patient work and a good deal of skill. If your material is good – and it will be if you've tried hard to produce genuine drama in your improvizations – then it will be worth the effort to spend time shaping and refining it for public presentation. The trouble is, of course, that the more satisfying your improvization has been, the better the material it has provided, the harder the job of choosing some parts of it for inclusion in the play and rejecting others. Some of the characters and scenes you were particularly fond of will have to be sacrificed in order to give the finished product those qualities of form and dramatic impact that go to make a good play out of a stimulating exercise in imagination. If you can't be tough with yourselves and exercise this painful kind of self-criticism, your play will run the risk of coming across as diffuse or even self-indulgent which, considering the amount of hard work that has gone into it, would probably be a great pity indeed. This being the case it would probably be a good idea to ask someone from outside the group to look at what you've made together and pay particular attention to any comments concerning the play's overall *shape* which are forthcoming! You'll probably find that it takes you just as long to fashion the final play for public presentation as it took to evolve the drama which gives it its life and makes it real and authentic.

Both the approaches described in the last chapter – working inwards towards the truth of someone else's play in order to make it your own, and outwards from the reality of your own dramatic experience as a means of communicating its truth to others – involve a good deal of hard work as well as having their own special problems. At the same time, it must be said that a church group possesses real advantages in the way of a shared sense of belonging and a common source of inspiration, over a company of actors and actresses called together from different directions in order to present a particular play, or a dramatic society where members have little in common besides the custom of meeting together once or twice a year and 'putting on a show'. It must also be said, with equal force, that no kind of play, whether it be 'tailor-made' or 'off-the-peg' will ever really strike home without the kind of personal involvement demanded by both these methods. Even if for one reason or another you feel you can't do everything I describe, I strongly recommend that you make the effort to have a go at some of it, at least. Find the bits you think you might be able to cope with, the parts that make sense to you, and work out your own version of them for your own use. In fact, of course, this is the only way that a book like this one can possibly be of use to anybody. You have to take the arts you can use and make them your own. Having said that, however, the fact remains that an awful lot of people miss a great deal of joy by their determination to 'play safe' – always a dangerous rule in life, but a simply disastrous one in art! A little courage, then; a little willingness to try something new – and I guarantee you'll be richly rewarded. Apart from which, taking this kind of risk together is marvellous for group cohesion. You'll find that everybody's sense of being personally committed to the task in hand is greatly enhanced. Remember, the two basic elements involved in making any kind of genuine theatre are determination and concentration. Indeed, these two things go together; and the best way of achieving them is by working as hard as you can together to develop your group's ability to develop its own natural creativity along the lines I suggest here.

As we saw in the last chapter, it's possible to make a play even if you haven't got a particular theme to develop when you actually start work. This is because the theme of every play, when you really get down to it, is the same. It is *personal relationships*. This is the place where you start, the basic subject matter of all theatre and drama, and the raw material out of which every play is fashioned. A more precise theme, an actual story, can be permitted to emerge later on. In fact, the impulse to protect yourself by working out in advance precisely what your play will be about, what its precise 'message' must be, can be a self-limiting one. It tends to result in improvized scenes which rapidly play themselves out without producing anything really practicable in the way of usable material. For 'usable' read 'stimulating for the imagination'. In a way that is both strange and fascinating, if you let the characters speak they will create the action. Just as the presence of people in a room suggests characters in a play, so the imagination of the actors and actresses representing these characters suggests the things they say, and this allows the play to develop in its own way. On the other hand, if you already know how it's all going to end – if it *has* to end up like that in order to get its message across – you invent dialogue in order to make everything fit your pre-determined intention, and the result is, I'm afraid, a string of cliché situations. Because nobody in the group is a talented playwright, you simply fall back on other people's ideas and reproduce scenes you're familiar with from any number of plays, films and TV soap operas you've seen in the past. You simply end up being boring!

The way out of this dilemma, which sooner or later confronts anyone who tries to create a play of their own, is to let the dialogue lead you along instead of dragging it along behind you as you try to catch up with the plot. This is extremely difficult to do, particularly for adults who don't want to appear foolish and so prefer to think before they speak, because it means you must put yourself in a frame of mind in which you're willing to speak first and think afterwards. You must say what your character feels like saying and shut up when he or she feels like shutting up. You must really trust your character and leave yourself entirely in his or her hands. If things seem to get out of hand (and they certainly will), you must let yourself go with the action and not try to force it back into familiar (cliché) territory. From time to time you'll find yourself drying up. This usually happens when you've been thinking too much and feeling too little, so that you've temporarily lost your spontaneity. When this happens, you must say so, and stop the action or withdraw from the scene, even if it means that everything grinds to a halt. When this happens, everyone has to start over again from the beginning – but this doesn't matter because the people who've been enjoying the way things have been going won't mind 'having another go' because they're surprised at their own creativity. If this doesn't turn out to be the case, it's a sign that people are tired – it's an extremely tiring activity, being creative – and a splendid opportunity to have a break. Don't go back to the play, leave it until you meet for the next session, and fill in the remaining time doing something more gentle and less taxing. You'll find people have been exhilarated by the challenge, however limited the results seem to you to have been. Almost certainly somebody will have got something out of it, and you'll find the group quite eager to have another go next time.

However, if it's only a case of a scene fizzling out or becoming stilted and repetitive, there's no need to finish the exercise altogether. In fact this is precisely what you should *not* do. When everything dries up, go back to the part that seemed to 'work' and move on from there. The only way to achieve something authentic is to keep trying. When something – anything – works, it must be allowed to continue, wherever it seems to be leading, because the improvizations which strike true and produce real feeling and involvement, however unexpected and outré they may be, are the material from which the final play will be constructed. If it isn't the play you intended, so much the worse for you – or so much the better, for the play you end up with will be an original piece of theatre rather than just another example of 'religious drama'. You could say it will be *more* religious, being in a very real way an act of courage and also of *faith;* faith that something of value to Christians is going to emerge from an exploration of human relationships which is rooted in a genuine personal experience of joy and pain.

While I'm writing this I'm involved, along with eight other people, in such an experience. Each Monday evening we meet as a group to try and create a play for ourselves along the lines I've described here. Up to now we've had two sessions together and there are three more to go before we finally finish. Whether we shall have achieved our object I don't know. Perhaps it's too early to judge. Anyhow, I've made notes of our progress up to now, and I intend to go on doing this so that I can include them here in order to give an idea of the kind of things which can happen when you set out to 'do-it-yourself' instead of going to the drama section of the library. There are four women and five men (including myself) in the group. The youngest are in their twenties and the oldest around sixty.

Session I

I didn't know who was going to turn up for this session. As it happened we had seven members of the group, making eight of us in all. I had worked with six of the others the previous year, reading and rehearsing a one-act play, using written texts to practise dialogue. Five were members of a local Methodist dramatic society, all of whom knew one another very well. The group contained two married couples, Andy and Joan and my wife and myself (Doreen and Roger). Apart from this there were Vernon, Phyllis and Terry, whom I knew from last year, and Peter, whom I didn't know, but most of the others did. The fact that we were more or less used to one another made it easier to get started, of course. First of all we did some warm-up exercises: flexing and releasing muscles, working in pairs and groups to develop trust through a sense of physical security (leaning backwards and forwards supporting and balancing each other and letting ourselves collapse into someone else's arms, etc.). After this we sat down in a circle and talked for a moment or two about ourselves, saying what had been happening to each of us since we last met. Peter didn't know me, of course, and was a bit embarrassed at being asked to do this, I think. His way of dealing with the situation was by adopting a slightly cynical and 'jokey' attitude to what was going on. We played an 'empathy game' in which people were encouraged to put themselves in each other's shoes to the extent of guessing likes and dislikes, then we went for a tea-break. The first half of the session had gone pretty well and I felt happy about the group's willingness to join in with one another (even Peter!).

In the second half of the session I asked everyone to sit round in a circle and talk about themselves again, this time 'in role'. I suggested we should assume the identity of a mutual support group of some kind who were going to meet from time to time in order to discuss any problems we happened to have. I was the leader and I knew each of them personally, but they didn't know one another, so they'd have to introduce themselves. Each person spoke for a few minutes, in the character they had chosen. Doreen as 'Sally' who had a drink problem but strongly objected to having anything to do with Alcoholics Anonymous, Vernon as 'Jake', a rather shy postman who said he preferred his job because he liked working by himself, Joan as 'Anne', who was bored sitting at home and wanted to meet some lively people. She said she'd joined the group hoping it would 'give her a laugh'. Terry assumed the role of 'Joe', a hamburger salesman who had a thriving business but wanted to discover a deeper meaning in life. Andy was 'Ian', a night-worker who wanted peace and quiet. He was troubled by his own anger towards the kids in the street who kept him awake. Peter was a troubled and aggressive youth with a disfiguring skin-condition which stopped him mixing with other people. His name was 'John' and he didn't know why he had come. The other member of the group, Phyllis, had had to leave after the first half of the session because of an important engagement. She told us she intended to come again next week, however. I was interested to see how readily the group fell into the spirit of the exercise. They seemed to have very little difficulty inventing these characters. Maybe I was lucky, or perhaps people like to do this kind of thing if they feel it's 'safe'. This part of the session went on for almost an hour, various characters expressing interest in one another's lives and revealing a high degree of empathy with the problems being described. I don't know how much of their own lives each brought to the role he or she was playing, but I'm reasonably sure that they weren't conscious of talking about themselves rather than in character, as the people they were portraying. I noticed that the group members who took most readily to this kind of role-play were those who had tended to have some difficulty projecting a character when reading from a script. My own experience in the role as the leader of the group also came as rather a surprise to me. I wasn't a bit like the kind of group leader I believe myself to be in 'real life'. This new person was more spontaneous and also more directive in his approach. Who could he be? I wondered. Perhaps this was the person I'd *like* to be! Immediately after the session I jotted down a note: 'I'm thinking about this new "group leader" who showed up tonight. It's a bit like this – in drama I want to say this or that, but I don't. Instead I find myself saying something (feeling something?) unexpected. It isn't that I say what I think the character would say; there's no time for thought. It's as if a new person emerges from my making the effort to leave my own "normal" state of reality in order to enter a new one. I know this isn't clear, but it's what I mean. To understand the effect you have to do it. *I* can say "I love you" on cue and the story would be neater if I did, but this new person can't, so he says or does something else instead, and the drama proceeds along its own lines, not mine. . .'

Session II (2 weeks later)

Because of the deep snow last week we weren't able to hold a session, and I'm feeling a bit anxious in case people have forgotten the characters they created the week before. We start as we did before, with some exercises. At the beginning of the session I happened to mention, merely in passing, the subject of psycho-drama. Peter picked this up, asking me what was psychodrama? I explained that it was a way of demonstrating interpersonal problems *in situ* by acting them out instead of just talking about them. This led to our dividing into pairs in order to play 'magic shop', a game in which people are encouraged to ask for an object, quality or skill which they most desire; they can have it on condition that they surrender some valued aspect of their present lives in return. After an improvized scene, hilarious in parts, involving a cast of characters arguing about a hole in the road, we got down to the main business of the evening. We'd decided to concentrate on the character of 'Joe', the hot-dog stand proprietor. Because we had already 'worked up' a situation in which someone was threatened with legal action unless they moved something (i.e. the hole in the road) Joe's play began with his having to close his stall down. The drama followed a rather tortuous and somewhat contrived path until Joe, having arranged to have the council official responsible mugged by two thugs, finally moved in with the lady who ran the newsagents stall on the railway station. The story was contrived because there were times when nobody could think what to do next and we had to fall back on someone's 'brilliant idea' for a solution to the problem of not having already worked out the ending in advance. On the other hand its tortuousness came from two scenes which really took off by themselves and led us into developments that were genuinely exciting because so unexpected. These scenes involved Peter and Phyllis. The slight feeling of alienation that Peter still carried gave a quality of authenticity to his portrayal of an underworld hoodlum bribed to set fire to the newsagent's stall for some nefarious purpose or other. Phyllis, who hadn't been present when the original characters were created, found herself 'put on the spot' with no ready-made ideas to fall back on. The two scenes already mentioned gained a good deal of their life from the spontaneity with which she rose to the challenge. However, I can't really claim that we came any closer to discovering a meaning in life this week. Next week we'll be approaching things from another character's viewpoint.

Session III

When we arrived in the theatre we found the stage was filled with a complicated arrangement of platforms, ready for the performance of *Godspell* which the school (whose theatre we're using) are presenting next month. I admit this threw me a little, because I'm used to working on an empty stage, but it's the kind of thing that frequently happens. The group didn't seem to mind at all, and sat in a long row dangling their legs over the edge of the new platform. We started with a group improvization exercise, involving everyone in an invented conversation in which nobody was allowed to 'block'. If they did, we all had to start again:

A   I told her she'd have to go!
B   But she's worked here for years.
C   Yes, but she's having an affair with the postman.
D   And he's married with seven kids. . .

At this point, E 'blocks' because he can't think of a way of keeping things going any longer:

E   Oh dear, what a pity!

This led into a game of 'masters and servants'. I'd brought a top hat along, and we used this to establish a chain of command according to which each member of the chain 'passed the buck' downwards:

A   Where did you put the balloons?
B   I'm awfully sorry sir, I gave them to C. (Turns to C) You there, where did you put the balloons?
C   The balloons? Yes, of course, right away, won't be a moment, chief. (Turns to D) Scum, fetch the balloons!
D   Oh yes, Master, always your humble servant, Master. (Grabs E by the throat) The balloons, d'you hear?   etc.

This game always gives rise to a good deal of hilarity, which has the effect of freeing people's inhibitions. When we went into the main improvization I withdrew from my previous role as the 'support group leader' so that the group could discuss things more freely. This gave 'Anne' and 'Bev' (Phyllis's 'character') the opportunity to express some negative feelings about the group in general and its leader in particular. 'Anne' said she was disappointed because it wasn't more fun, and 'Bev' said she thought it was boring, as well. Someone suggested that they should all adjourn to the pub to talk things over, and they moved up on to the central part of the platform to set up a pub scene. At this point 'Sally' objected, saying she couldn't go into a pub because of her drink problem, and 'Anne' offered to go out with her for the evening, 'Just the two of us'. After a scene in which 'Anne' informed her truculent husband that she was going out 'with a friend', attention moved to a pub scene in which two 'strangers' ('Anne' and 'Sally') came into the bar, and drew ribald comments from the regulars, one of whom became over-familiar with 'Anne', causing 'Sally' to intervene. One of the men at the bar recognized her as a well-known former 'lush', with the result that she fled from the pub and ran into the park. 'Anne' followed her and tried to comfort her. At this point things began to lose something of their impetus. I intervened, suggesting that 'Anne' might be worried in case her friend tried to commit suicide. 'Sally' resisted this suggestion and made some strong comments about people who did things like that. . .

The highlights of the session were definitely the scene in the pub and the one in the park. When, as an outsider, I tried to introduce 'dramatic interest' I only succeeded in interfering with the life developing in the play itself. The session itself was somewhat bland; we were still recovering from the hilarity of the earlier part. Perhaps I should have postponed this until the end, when the serious business of the session was over. Whether or not we shall be able to produce any kind of viable theatre from all this remains to be seen. It has certainly had its dramatic moments, however. Meanwhile, I'm interested to see how 'Joe's desire to 'find a meaning in life' led him into an episode marked mainly by violence, while 'Anne's' need to 'have a bit of fun' developed into a story about friendship and loyalty.

Session IV

This was our first session for three weeks, and I was a bit anxious in case we'd lost the thread of the characters, and situations we had been developing in the first three sessions. I needn't have worried, however. We started with some warm-up exercises, and then played a game in which people put one another into various poses, 'sculpting' them as if they were statues, first of all expressing what the 'sculptor' considered to be the least characteristic pose for his subject, and then going on to the most characteristic one. When everyone had had a turn at being both 'sculptor' and 'statue', we stood in a circle and held hands, so that we could pass a message round by squeezing the hand of our neighbour on one side as soon as we felt whoever was standing next to us on the other side squeeze ours. When we had got the squeeze travelling really fast round the circle, we relaxed and simply stood holding hands, concentrating on the feeling of warmth being transmitted from person to person around the ring. All this gave rise to a good deal of laughter, which got us into the right mood for working together on the play. The rest of the session was a bit static as far as bodies were concerned, but imaginations were certainly active. I began by asking each group member to remind the rest of us about the character he or she had created in our original exercise about the 'support group'. How could we develop the work we'd been doing during the last few weeks into some kind of play? We thought at first about the possibility of building on the idea of a group of people with individual personal problems who were all brought together by force of circumstance into the same place, at the same time: something along the lines of the plane and train 'disaster' movies frequently shown on TV. This idea was soon dropped, Phyllis pointing out the essential banality of contriving a situation in which everybody's personal tragedy was miraculously transformed into triumph by a single cataclysmic event – disaster in more than one sense. The group then decided to concentrate on the three characters whose lives had been touched on in the main improvizations, Sally, Anne, and Joe. The plot which eventually emerged drew much of its inspiration from the pub scene created during the last session. The situation which centred around Sally seemed to attract most interest from the group, and Anne's attempt to help her friend seemed to contain the germ of something that might perhaps be developed. For a time at least, everyone's imagination went into top-gear, and the tea-break was postponed. . .

The scenario which eventually emerged was something like this. (Sc.1) Anne, a restless housewife wants to try and help Sally, whom she has recently met. Sally is wrestling with a drink problem, and Anne has arranged to meet her this evening and take her to a coffee-bar to 'talk things over'. Jim, Anne's husband, thinks his wife is wasting her time trying to help down-and-outs, and argues with her; she should stay at home with him and watch TV 'like a proper wife'. Anne leaves to meet Sally. (Sc.2) Because they can't find anywhere to have coffee, Anne and Sally go into a pub for a soft drink. Some of the locals recognize Sally and begin to taunt her. Anne turns on them in anger, but Sally has run out of the pub in despair. (Sc.3) Anne catches up with Sally in the park. Sally is suicidal, so Anne takes her along to see Joe, who runs the hamburger stall near the park gates, and who has a reputation for being a philosopher. Anne goes home, leaving Sally at Joe's stall. (Sc.4) Joe has gone back to Sally's flat. She said she couldn't face going there alone, and Joe can see why. While Joe is clearing out all the bottles, Sally's daughter Bev arrives with her boyfriend Ziggy. They are off to an all-night disco, and won't stay. (Sc.5) Next morning. Joe has slept on Sally's sofa. He's very anxious about his stall, but before he leaves he rings Anne in order to get her to come round and keep an eye on Sally, who's still talking about suicide. Ziggy and Bev return to find Sally sitting alone, clutching her bottle of tablets. They storm out again in disgust. In the street, however, Bev has a moment of remorse and rings up the hospital. (Sc.6) Anne wants to go and look after

Sally. Jim is protective towards his wife and won't let her out of the house. (Sc.7) The doctor arrives at Sally's flat. He tells her he can't take her into hospital because she's only threatening suicide and hasn't actually taken the tablets. He'll send the Community Nurse round later in the day, or perhaps tomorrow. Sally says she'll be all right, Anne's on the way. In the final sequence (Sc.8) each of the characters who has been involved in Anne's attempt to help Sally speaks directly to the audience, explaining his or her attitude; first the doctor, then Bev and Ziggy, Joe and finally Jim. They've all done everything they could. Anne simply sits and weeps. During this sequence Sally moves slowly up-stage to the open window of her twelfth-storey flat. When she reaches the edge, the lights go out.

The session ended with a sense that something had really been achieved. It had been a corporate effort, no single person having been responsible for the final story, although the general idea for the climax at the end, which gave the play its 'shape', came from Peter ('the doctor') and Doreen ('Sally'). As we only had one more meeting planned, we decided to spend it rehearsing the play as it now stood. I volunteered to draw up a skeleton script, putting down the gist of each scene in the form of a few lines of essential dialogue, which the cast could improvize around.

Session V

This was a more-or-less straightforward rehearsal session. It was hard to keep the scenes from becoming too long, as people seemed to want to go on improvizing indefinitely. (It's a good idea to plan a 'final line' for a scene, because this gives the actors an excuse to stop!) We used a tape-recorder to record the scenes so that a proper working script could be put together from the improvized dialogue. When the rehearsal finished, all that had to be done to make the play workable could be carried out in a more leisurely fashion by a co-ordinator who would simply organize the spoken dialogue into its final form. This I volunteered to do.

At the time of writing, the play has still to be properly rehearsed and performed. However, it *is* a play – and it's ours! It may not appear to be a particularly 'religious' play. On the other hand, it was conceived by a group of people who are all sincere Christians. The aim throughout was to create something that *felt true about life*, rather than something which people considered 'suitable for church'.

However, we shall do it in church if we get the chance. I shall be saying more about the kinds of play which are suitable for church presentation in Chapter 6.

Note

By far the best book I have come across about improvization is Keith Johnstone *Impro*, Methuen 1981. I recommend this enthusiastically to anybody interested in drama. Do try to read it if you can get hold of it. The chapter on 'Masks and Trance' is particularly fascinating.

5   Strictly Practical

Obviously, if you're doing a play, you've got to be both heard and seen. In church this can be quite a serious problem. Churches tend to be vast and echoing. They have rows of pillars which obscure the view, or narrow chancels so that you find yourself gazing at an altar which seems to be at the other end of a long, dark tunnel, or close ranks of fixed pews just where the stage should be. Anyone who has ever taken a play into a series of different churches will know, too, that every one has its own unique hazards, things you never expected at all until you arrived and started to get ready for the performance. It's a challenge, certainly – but it can also be quite a headache. The aim of this chapter, then, is to look at ways of overcoming some of the more familiar hurdles.

1.   Being heard

Speaking very loudly isn't any solution. The sound simply bounces back, echoing from the heights of the gothic clerestory or booming away in deep cavities above the Victorian gallery. On the other hand, it's likely to be a large church and your voice has a long way to go, a vast area of empty space to penetrate. You can't just talk as if you were holding an ordinary conversation in somebody's living-room. The difficulty of being heard in the quiet passages of a play has to be taken into account everywhere you may happen to be performing, in theatres as well as churches; but it's considerably worse in churches. It's even harder here than outside in the open air, because of the built-in echo and the tendency of the architecture to swallow any sound you make.

However, these problems are to do with volume, rather than quality, of sound. Although volume and intensity of sound are important, they are by no means the only things involved in dramatic communication; and they are less important when you're acting in church than they are in a theatre – which, after all, is specially designed for plays. In circumstances where too much sound is counterproductive, you have to use other ways of getting your meaning across. These are correct *pitch, pace* and *rhythm, clarity of speech,* and *facial expression.*

First of all, however, before you can do anything else you have to overcome the nervousness that people feel when they're expected to perform in unfamiliar surroundings. However accustomed you may be to acting in rooms, or even on stages, performing in a church always seems a bit odd the first time you do it. A good way of overcoming this is by choral speaking. Reciting a poem or a passage from a play in unison almost always has the effect of building confidence within the group, because individuals who are too shy to speak and move about in a free and uninhibited way as solo performers are reassured by having other people around them who are all doing the same thing, so that if they happen to make a mistake it isn't so obvious. The more confidence, the fewer mistakes! Speaking to music is even more effective in countering nervousness, because it makes it much easier to keep in rhythm, and produces a sense of enjoyment which is perhaps more valuable than anything else – as we saw when we were discussing the various exercises aimed at building group cohesion mentioned earlier. Speaking together in time to the music is a way of using the strength of a group both literally, in terms of stronger sound and more definite rhythm and metaphorically, with regard to greater relaxation and sense of co-operation among individuals. Generally speaking, poetry is better than prose. One of the choruses from *Murder in the Cathedral* would be ideal for this purpose, or you could use a chorus from one of the Greek classical plays.

Pitch Choral speaking is also a good way of establishing the correct level of pitch in an unfamiliar building. 'Pitch' is defined as 'the degree of acuteness of tone'. It has something to do with the actual volume of sound, but more to do with its definition. It's better to think of it as the way in which your voice interacts with the architecture of the building. Once you have discovered the right pitch you can speak as loudly as you want without producing the annoying distortion of sound that is the first thing you notice when you try to make yourself heard in a large church building. You can also speak much more quietly than you might expect, and still be heard at the back of the nave or up in the gallery. This is very important. If your performance is to have the variety it needs in order to express the whole range of feeling that any play demands of its actors you must be able to speak softly as well as loudly. This is why I usually start rehearsals in an unfamiliar building by getting everybody to experiment in order to see how loudly they have to whisper in order to be heard by somebody standing at the furthest point from the acting area.

Tone itself is very important, of course. Your voice must be expressive as well as audible, so you have to spend some time concentrating on trying to extend the range flexibility of the sounds you produce. The Oxford Dictionary defines tone as 'the modulation of voice to express emotion', and actors are accustomed to making use of a whole range of exercises in order to make their use of language more tonally expressive. Some of the ones that I have found useful are given here:

1. Practise using the lower part of the rib-cage to produce your voice correctly. The strength and impact of the sound you produce mustn't be provided by the throat and larynx, but by the diaphragm. This is the muscular partition separating the thorax from the abdomen, which acts as a kind of bellows when you expand and contract your rib-cage.

2. Try closing your mouth and humming as loudly as you can, up and down the scale. Gradually open your lips and make a steady sound. When this begins to falter, cut it off, draw a breath and start again. See if you can keep your sound going a bit longer each time.

3. Inhale, stretching your ribs, for a count of five; hold your breath for five beats; exhale for five beats. Repeat the exercise inhaling for ten beats, holding for ten, exhaling for ten; gradually extend the time spent inhaling, holding your breath, expelling the air. This is particularly good for learning breath control, which is essential for good tonal modulation. You can also practise gradually increasing the number of words you can say in a sentence.

4. Practise how to keep your tone pure when sustaining a particular sound, starting with closed lips giving a sustained mmm sound, then opening the lips slightly and lifting the tongue to the back of the teeth to produce nnn, then open the lips and pushing them out for oooooh, stretching them for eeeeeh, widening them for aaaaah, etc.

5. Finally, here is an exercise designed for clarity and flexibility

of speech which I've found very useful when it comes to speaking rapidly while remaining audible – not always an easy thing to try to do. It involves using consonants and vowels together, and you have to do it as quickly as possible, running through the list of vowels and pairing them with various consonants: 'manamah, menemeh, minimih, monomoh, munumuh, nananah, neneneh, nininih, nononoh, nununuh. . .' (continue with sasasah, tatatah, vavavah, etc., increasing in speed while trying always to preserve clarity.)

Pace This is not to be confused with sheer speed, being closer to animation and also to rhythm. A speech which has 'pace' may in fact contain plenty of actual pauses; but it will be characterized by an overall 'shape' so that it hangs together in an expressive way, and moves purposefully onwards despite changes in tone and alterations in speed of delivery. This, too, is connected with breath control, because once the pace of breathing becomes confused and irregular, words tend to get jumbled together. Also the syllables which follow immediately after an unintentional pause, one which has happened simply because breath has run out, tend to be quicker and louder than the rest of the speech. It's as if you're trying to make up for lost time. Just as slow speech needs a good even flow of breath from the lungs in order to sustain the volume and level of sound, rapid speech needs regular breathing in order to stop you falling over yourself in the effort to communicate a sense of urgency.

Clarity This can be developed in a straightforward way by reading aloud at various speeds and degrees of loudness and softness while paying strict attention to enunciation of vowels and consonants. However, clarity of meaning is something rather more complex than this. If you listen to a really good actor you'll notice that he (or she) has the ability to capture and hold the audience's attention by changes of tone which precisely reflect changes in meaning and intention. Dramatic clarity depends on the expression of meaning by modulation of voice and articulation, which simply means the expressive 'shape' given to words and phrases. Good dramatic speech is marked by a high degree of variety of pace, tone, inflexion; it is this that keeps us alert and attentive, so that, far from having a confusing or overwhelming effect, the variety of impressions we receive actually adds to the clarity of the meaning which comes across. Changes of thought and feeling within a speech, the onset of new ideas and the animation involved in developing a particular argument, must all be expressed by changes in intonation, the use of pauses, variations in rhythm, etc. in order to do any kind of justice to the playwright's intention. This is something that every actor acknowledges, of course. The trouble is that intention and execution don't always go hand in hand. It's amazing how dull even the most exciting and stimulating speech can sound when delivered by an inexperienced actor. This is particularly true if the speech is long and detailed. One of the best ways of approaching this problem from a technical point of view is to learn how to use what Pamela Keily calls 'a new voice'. This doesn't necessarily mean a new tone of voice, although it can, and frequently does, involve a change of inflexion. What is really required here is a new start. In other words, you begin this part of what you have to say as if you were starting a new speech altogether. You use a vocal inflexion that communicates quite clearly that this is a new idea or feeling, or a new stage in the development of your argument. If you do this, you'll find that the tone of your voice changes expressively, in tune with the development of ideas and feelings contained in the speech. Each time you use a 'new voice' you draw the audience's attention to what you're actually saying and make your meaning clearer to them. This is something we do naturally enough, of course, in real life. In real life, however, we don't always know precisely what we're going to say next, so that new ideas come as a bit of a surprise to us, and this surprise is reflected in our tone of voice. If we are to act realistically in plays, we must learn how to reproduce the effect on stage; and this means learning the occasions on which a 'new voice' is required at the same time as learning our lines. This helps to improve our performance in other ways as well, because it anchors our concentration within the play itself, by continually calling our attention away from the effort to try and remember what we're supposed to say next, and back to what we're saying and feeling at the time. Anything which increases our concentration on the immediate situation within the play makes things more real for the audience as well.

As an example of the kind of thing I mean, here is the beginning of Alec McCowen's solo performance of St Mark's Gospel. I have marked the points where a 'new voice' is used with a stroke, thus: / This doesn't necessarily mean a pause, but it always signifies a kind of vocal 'change of gear'. As you can see, these points aren't always situated at the beginning of sentences or phrases, but occur wherever a new idea takes hold of the speaker. Sometimes he continues in the same voice for several phrases, in order to show that what you'd expect to be happening is actually taking place (as in v.5):

1. The beginning of the gospel of Jesus Christ, the / Son of God;
2. / As it is written in the prophets, Behold, I send my messenger before thy face, which shall prepare thy way before thee.
3. The voice of one / crying in the wilderness / Prepare ye the way of the Lord, / make his paths straight.
4. / John / did baptize in the wilderness, and / preach the / baptism of repentance for the remission of sins.
5. / And there went out unto him all the land of Judea, and they of Jerusalem, and were all baptized of him in the river Jordan, confessing their sins.
6. / And John was / clothed with camel's hair, and with a girdle of a skin about his loins; and he / did eat locusts and wild honey;
7. / And preached, saying / There cometh one mightier than I after me, the latchet of whose shoes I am not worthy to stoop down and unloose.

Notice how many changes of voice occur in v.4, the most important verse from the point of view of the meaning of the extract. Keeping hold of an audience's attention for the length of an entire Gospel is quite a feat. Alec McCowen does it so brilliantly that it succeeds even on tape, when you're not able to see the actor's gestures and facial expression. (This tape is worth getting hold of, if you haven't got it already.)

If we are to be both heard and understood, we must concentrate not only on the quality and quantity of the sound we produce but on its ability to convey the meaning we intend. As the second of these things concerns our awareness of the play itself rather than our consciousness of the way we're performing it, we must find ways which help us to improve our vocal skills while deepening our understanding of the role we're playing. One way to do this would be by using passages from the play in order to practise voice production. The only really effective way, however, is to practise the technical aspects so thoroughly that when the time comes to perform the play for an audience, we can almost forget them. I say almost because there's always part of an actor's awareness which must be busy monitoring his performance, making sure that what he's doing and saying is really audible and visible from the back of the gallery. It's as if part of you is up in the gods, watching and listening to yourself down there on the stage. With practice, this becomes second nature, so that you hardly notice it happening and simply concentrate on what you're doing on stage. But it does take practice; and I can't stress too strongly that effective communication in the theatre depends on developing this ability to judge how well you can be heard without letting it intrude on the quality of your involvement within the play itself. If you make a mental picture of the people who are sitting furthest away from you and keep this in the back of your mind without letting it intrude into the foreground of your conscious awareness, you'll find that even when you drop your voice they can still hear you. In a strange kind of way, your concentration on what's happening to you in the play actually makes you easier to hear. If you're really *living* the lines you're saying you can actually whisper and still be heard. On the other hand it's as well to warn the audience that they're going to have to listen more intently. As with sudden changes in tone, surprising drops in the volume of sound produced have the effect of commanding attention. If it suddenly gets quiet, people find themselves listening more intently. It's no use doing this slowly; if your voice gradually gets softer, the audience will begin to lose interest as it becomes harder and harder to hear what you're saying. You have to do it abruptly; and having done it you must remember to speak more slowly in order to give them time to change gear and start listening all the harder. No one who heard him will ever forget the way that Alec McCowen delivered those marvellous lines of Richard II: 'a little, little grave, An unknown grave'. The words were only whispered, and yet they penetrated to the last row of the gallery at the Old Vic Theatre in Waterloo Road.

Facial expression You can hear people much better if you can see their faces, because hearing and sight are closely interconnected. This certainly doesn't mean that you have to stand facing the audience and address your fellow players without looking them in the eye. If you're talking to someone, then turn towards them as you would normally do, but let the audience see what's written on your face by turning away in their direction when you've said what you want to say or heard what you wanted to hear. After all, that's what you usually do when you're not on-stage – you don't stand staring away from people all the time, nor do you fix them with an unwavering glare. If you react quite naturally when someone speaks to you, you'll find yourself looking away from them slightly in order to take in what they've just said. If it isn't anything very important, this will only be a slight movement of the eyes; but if what they said 'gets through' to you in any way you instinctively move your head, or even your body, away. If you practise the following short snatch of dialogue, you'll see what I mean:

She: I did it because I love you. If you're always doing things for *me,* it doesn't give me a chance to do anything for *you,* does it?

He: (getting the point at last): Oh yes; I never thought of it like that. . .

As he says this line, he turns away from her. He doesn't turn away *in order* to say the line, but the 'emotional charge' contained by the line actually turns him away, so that he starts to speak as he begins to turn. It's a kind of emotional reflex, and it happens all the time. What you have to do when you're acting is make sure that it happens in the right direction. When you turn away in order to think about what's going on, or when the emotion itself turns you away, let it be towards the audience, so they can see whatever is written on your face. You don't have to show them. Just let them see. Bodily movement is also very expressive. Indeed it can be even more articulate than facial expression. Funnily enough it seems to work best in the opposite direction; that is, when someone turns *away* from the audience or actually stands with their back to them. All of this leads into the whole business of –

2. Being seen

I said that hearing and sight are closely linked, which means that you aren't likely to pick up subtle vocal inflexions if you're seated behind a pillar and can't see the stage at all. Unfortunately this is the kind of thing that frequently happens when plays are produced in churches: the need to avoid architectural obstacles in the shape of pillars, fonts, pulpits and rood-screens concentrates the area available to the audience into a long narrow strip down the centre of the nave corresponding to little more than a third of the actual width of the church. From this vantage point, you can see as far as the altar, with the chancel step conveniently providing a kind of platform for the actors. Unfortunately, the platform isn't any wider than the area in which the audience is sitting, because of the presence of fixed choir-stalls. On the other hand the space in front of the choir stalls provides a wide but rather shallow acting area stretching across the church into which a stage could be inserted, although in most cases there would be very little room between the edge of the stage and the front row of pews; and you'd still have the problem of those pillars. In fact, the alternatives seem to be not seeing some of the actors because others are standing in front of them in an acting area which is deep but narrow (i.e. between the choir stalls), or not seeing some of them because the architecture itself blocks off parts of an area which is wide but shallow. From the actors' point of view, both alternatives are almost equally restricting; on a wide, shallow stage you can't concentrate the action, so that you feel as though you're miles away from everyone else, while a space which is narrow and deep gives nobody any room to spread themselves and 'use the stage' in order to express emotion by means of movement (after all, you can't always be performing Sartre's *Huis Clos!*)

Figure I gives a good idea of the problem. Admitted not all Gothic churches are quite as bad for plays as this one is, but it certainly demonstrates some of the worst things that can happen to you. The best solution here would be to set up your stage so that it takes up all the space indicated. If you rope off the pews along the dotted lines and use the central part of the nave only for the audience most people will have a reasonably good view. Unfortunately, the stage will have to be as high as the backs of the pews, so that you can see the actors' feet; generally speaking, however, it's better to keep the acting area reasonably low, about 2'6" from floor level, in order to avoid the impression that people are acting on a kind of narrow shelf. In *Figure II* the problem is simpler. This church has been re-ordered to accommodate a nave altar. Obviously a good deal depends on whether or not this is movable. If it is, the whole area marked (1) provides a splendid stage, and because of the space between this and the pews, the platform on which the altar is positioned removes the necessity for any kind of stage.

Figure III illustrates a Free Church which would be ideal for plays. It must be admitted, though, that Free Church settings aren't always as good as this one, although they often provide a series of levels on which to act, and of course they don't have fixed altars.

In churches which have chairs instead of pews, the problem is much easier, because you can move things around and design the kind of acting area that you'd actually choose to have, instead of having to make do with something which is largely imposed on you

Figure I

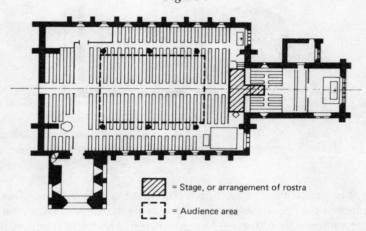

= Stage, or arrangement of rostra

= Audience area

Figure II

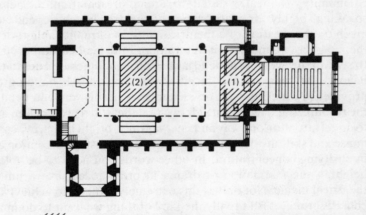

= Acting areas (1) Orthodox arrangement (church with fixed pews)
(2) Theatre-in-the-round (church with moveable seating)

= Rostra for audience seated 'in the round'

= Audience area for fixed pews

Figure III

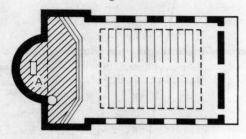

///// = Acting area. This will, almost certainly
require the use of rostra on
order to give more height to
the area within the apse. (A)

by the architecture. The church illustrated in *Figure II* may also be
adapted for the presentation of a play-in-the-round. That is, with
the audience seated around a central arena. The kind of drama that
we have been mainly concerned with in this book, drama which
emerges from the life of, and expresses the spirit of, a Christian
community, is ideally suited to arena presentation. Generally
speaking, highly 'dramatic' types of theatre, which depend very
much on the creation of a theatrical illusion of reality able to seize
the imagination and hold it in thrall until the final curtain drops at
the end of the evening, depend largely on techniques of presentation
beyond the range of the facilities that any church building can
provide. In order to work on an audience in this way you need all
the resources and technical aids of a real theatre: a proscenium arch
to direct attention one way and one way only, bright lights, evocative
music and skilfully designed sets aimed at focussing perception and
intensifying concentration. In other words you need to be able to
heighten the fascination of drama in order to achieve a unique
theatrical magic. Not only is this extremely difficult to achieve in a
church setting, it isn't really the kind of thing we want to do in any
case. We are after something much simpler and less technical. Our
purpose is to invite the audience to share in an experience which is
genuinely 'life-like' and able to attract the power of imagination on
which all drama depends; but we wouldn't want people to be forced
to participate by the sheer weight of our technical expertise, even if
such a thing were possible. If you've got something to share, you

don't want people to feel themselves brow-beaten into accepting it. On the contrary, you want them left free to choose. Theatre-in-the-round is a much gentler way of sharing drama with people than presenting it on a platform in front of them.

For one thing, because they have an overall view of the acting area, the audience can see much better what's happening among the actors. This means that it's more difficult to draw people's attention in any particular direction at the expense of events taking place somewhere else in the drama. This doesn't mean that important points get missed, simply that everything happening in the play is experienced as important, and the really dramatic events have to make themselves felt in their own way and at their own time. The effect is slower than proscenium theatre but somehow deeper and more real. Theatre-in-the-round preserves the truth of drama from some of the more contrived and artificial elements of theatre: and this makes it an easier medium for technically inexperienced actors and actresses. For one thing, you don't have to be so skilled at making sure you can be heard and seen by everybody in the theatre. There's always part of the audience who can see and hear you quite easily, and when you're acting in an arena it's amazing how rapidly the news gets around. People who can't actually see you, and may even have missed what you said, pick the point up from people's faces with an ease you wouldn't believe possible unless you've experienced it yourself.

The other thing which is very helpful for a beginner is the feeling of security which comes from being literally surrounded by people who are eager to participate in the drama as well as you, and want to give you all the support they possibly can. Even the terror of having to make your entrance into the middle of an audience instead of just in front of them (which is bad enough in all conscience!) is swept away, once you're in the arena, by the tide of support and encouragement which meets you there and keeps you buoyed up for as long as the play lasts.

Generally speaking, too, audiences prefer to be in a higher position than the actors. They like to see what's going on without having to crane their necks or keep adjusting their position in order to secure a clear view between the heads of the people sitting in the row in front. This is worth remembering even if you don't decide to experiment with actual theatre-in-the-round. If there happens to be a raised area in the church, it would be better to seat the audience on it and use the ground level for the stage. For example, in *Figure III* the audience could be arranged in Area 'A', looking down the church, while the players perform in area 'B'. You'd need some extra platforms for this idea to work properly; but these would be used to bank up the auditorium rather than to raise the acting area itself.

In any case, movable platforms are much better than trying to work with staging constructed as a single long unit. The kind of thing I mean is what actors and stage managers call a rostrum. This is a large box with a folding frame and a removable top. You can make your own stage by putting a row of rostra next to one another, or you can arrange them in any way you want to make the best use of whatever space is available. *Figure IV* shows the use of rostra in order to turn the chancel of our own hospital church into an arena stage. As you can see, this is only a semi-arena. However, this is a much better arrangement than using the nave as the auditorium,

Figure IV

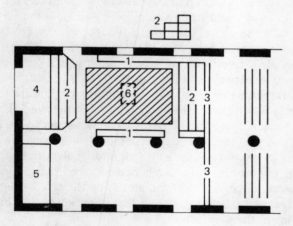

1. Choir Stalls
2. Arrangement of rostra (see inset)
3. Step up from nave
4. Platform beneath E. window
5. Organ
6. Moveable altar

///// = Acting area

Figure V

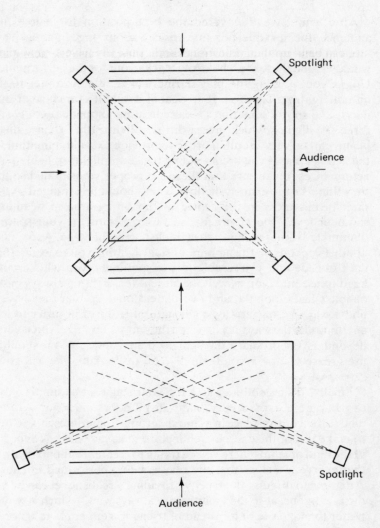

because the audience can really see what's going on in the acting area.

After you have discovered the best position for actors and audience, the next question that arises is about stage lighting. This, too, can be a problem, because churches usually have a great many windows, and these can't be easily blacked out for the performance. Unless you're doing the play during winter, it's far better to use natural lighting. There's a good deal of it, and it's far cheaper than floods and spots. Sometimes a basic lighting kit made up of two or three floodlights, which give a diffused light rather than a direct beam, can be very useful in order to provide extra illumination for the acting area. If you are intending to use spotlights to light up the actors' faces, make sure that these are properly positioned so that they don't cast too much shadow. They should be arranged so that their beams cross in the centre of the acting area at head-and-shoulder level (see *Figure V*). In this way most of your space is illuminated rather than just the middle part of the stage. As to make-up, this depends on the amount of stage lighting you're using. If it's dark outside and you're able to use spotlights, you will certainly need to use make-up as well, because direct lighting always makes people's faces look flat and two-dimensional, so that they have to find a way of exaggerating their natural features in order to look anything like the way they do when they aren't on stage. But if you're depending on ordinary daylight to light your set, you shouldn't use grease-paint, or you'll simply end up looking like actors and actresses!

Finally, it's a good idea to keep your stage set as simple as you can. Large pieces of scenery, 'naturalistic' doors and window frames, tend to look out-of-place in a church setting. Sometimes, it's possible to make use of the church architecture in a way which is evocative of the kind of atmosphere you're trying to create. Remember always that everyone knows that the play is being performed in church. Attempts to disguise the fact by providing a realistic set can be very distracting, because the architecture always wins – which is why it's better to make use of it instead of trying to get people to ignore it. The kind of truth you're aiming at doesn't depend on your ability to create a ready-made illusion. The imaginative part is something that emerges from the drama itself, and not from the scenery or the costumes, which can distract almost as much as they help. Besides which, the church setting is there to provide a background of a metaphorical kind quite apart from any practical purpose it may serve by fitting in with the scene you're creating. If you want your audience to forget that they are in a church altogether, perhaps you shouldn't be using the building at all!

Notes

Alec McCowen's solo performance of St Mark's Gospel is available in a two cassette pack, recorded by 'Bookassettes', K4 68025, mono. There are several very good books on voice production available. I recommend Arthur Hewlett, *Think About the Voice,* Buckland Press 1971. The classic work on arena theatre is Stephen Joseph, *Theatre in the Round,* Barrie and Rockliff 1967. Other useful books are two by Francis Reid, *The Lighting Handbook* and *The Staging Handbook,* both published by A. & C. Black, 1981, 1982.

6 'Mysteries' and 'Moralities'

In the spring of 1980 the various schools, colleges and amateur dramatic societies in and around the ancient Yorkshire city of Wakefield joined together to perform the Townley Cycle of mediaeval mystery plays, which are closely associated with this area. This was a considerable undertaking: people said that it was the first time all the plays had been acted together since the end of the Middle Ages. It called for a good deal of co-operative effort, as may be imagined. Each drama group was allocated a play of its own, just as, in the old days, the individual plays which made up the cycle 'belonged' to different trade guilds within the city. It was great fun to put the plays on again after so many centuries, and everyone involved showed a great deal of enthusiasm.

It wasn't all that difficult, either, because the texts came across to us as surprisingly relevant to life in today's world. I suppose you could say that we learned our lines easily because we were so familiar with the story. . .

The hard part came in the actual performance. If you're used to a 'proper' theatre, even one which has to double as a school assembly hall, it comes as quite a shock to find yourself required to perform in the open air; and if you've always had a nice wide stage at your disposal, trying to act on the back of a cart can be a testing experience, both for your skill and your temper. I suppose I was lucky, having had practice in this sort of thing when I worked with a theatre company specializing in doing plays in village schools. Once, I remember, we toured round the London parks with an open-air production. But even in the parks the audience sat on chairs to watch the play; whereas here, outside the cathedral on a busy April Saturday morning, the townspeople simply went about their business as usual, doing their weekend shopping, greeting their friends, standing around in groups and chatting. Sometimes they glanced in our direction. Usually they just went on gossiping. This really was something new, even for me. I'd been a strolling player, certainly, but I'd never had a strolling audience. I began to understand a little of what it must be like to be a busker. I was certain the mediaeval tradesmen-actors never had it as bad as this. In those days the combination of religious enthusiasm and guild loyalty must have made things very much easier.

In the event, it was the play itself that rescued us. Our play was 'The Resurrection of Jesus'. With a story like that it's difficult for actors to fail! What was actually happening to us on the platform, the situation within the play itself, took hold of our own minds and moved our hearts, so that after a bit we forgot our audience – or lack of one – as we re-created the circumstances of Holy Saturday and Easter Day, letting ourselves be taken up by the wonder of it all, losing ourselves, and our self-consciousness, in the task of establishing through the power of shared imagination something of the quality of the disciples' experience as they greeted the risen Lord. Very soon, with that part of an actor's mind which always remains detached from the business of doing and feeling within the world of the play, we began to sense a subtle change in atmosphere within the surrounding environment. Something was beginning to happen not only on the platform, but among the passers-by. After a bit, there was definitely less movement and conversation out front. People stopped talking and started looking. It was as if they too were being drawn in by what was happening in the play. They were starting to forget the price of stewing steak and beginning slowly to take account of what was happening to Jesus.

Something *was* happening, both on stage and in the audience. The audience was starting to be an audience instead of merely a crowd. Things were beginning to 'gel'. But it was never easy. You could never just relax and enjoy yourself, for as soon as you became consciously aware of the audience's reaction to the play you had to concentrate twice as hard on forgetting it. You had to do this or the whole thing began to go to pieces again. You certainly couldn't just stand there and belt it out at them – they simply drifted away, first mentally, and then physically. Actors often talk about losing their audience; there in the cathedral precinct, it was suddenly much more than an expressive metaphor – it was true in the most literal way. People would concentrate on the play just so long as you did; the more you lost yourself in the action, the more they helped you to do so. The concentration was contagious, moving out from the platform to the heterogeneous collection of individuals standing around out there, drawing them closer to one another and to the actors, making them participants in the action rather than just spectators. As the play reached its climax you could actually feel the group of shoppers, strollers and business people up there with you in the play. But once you lost your concentration you lost theirs too, and when this happened the whole event soon lapsed into unreality. It was as if it was what was taking place between you and them that made it all real; and yet what was taking place was simply the play, the actual story of the Resurrection of God's Son. It was *the play* that was doing it – the play that held us in its grip and forced us to surrender to its life-giving message.

This, of course, is what happens in every really authentic kind of theatre – imagination is powerfully focussed on the living experience of men and women. It came across so very strikingly here because the interplay of story and character in these plays exerts a tremendous pull on the imagination of believers and unbelievers alike. Apart from this, however, doing a play in the street, in the very middle of the human activity you're engaged in commenting upon in the play, is bound to be an effective way of delivering a theatrical message. Here is an example of modern 'street theatre' which I took part in some years ago:

The Trial of Trimmer Trend

Scene I (Enter Mr Trend between armed guards, handcuffed. He is marched to the courtroom. Narrator steps forward.)

Narrator: Behold the devilish dilemma of Mr Trend! (drums) Descry his dark, desperate and damnable plight! (drums) Disembogue your disapproval at the distinct divagations of one who – crass criminal – connived to concuss and confute his comminating conscience!! (drums) Now he faces his dreadful deserts (He is handed a bowl of rice pudding). Thank you. And another, more dreadful desert, yes friends, he faces his damnation!! (drums) (etc.)

Scene II (Narrator produces a sign '10 YEARS AGO')

Trend: For the last time, will you shut up?

Conscience: I'm only doing my job.

Trend: Well, will you go and do your job somewhere nice and quiet, please, where I can't hear you.

Conscience: You don't seem to understand. I am your *conscience*, Mr Trend.

Trend: As you have said before. Now run along, there's a good conscience.

Conscience: I'm not a good conscience, that's just the trouble, in fact, I'm rapidly becoming a bad conscience. Look at this. (Shows heavy sack marked 'GUILT'.) I've had to carry this around with me for the last year and a half, ever since that shady business deal of yours with Sham Enterprises Ltd. It's more than I can take (etc.)

(Murray Watts, used by permission)

Space doesn't permit me to include any more of the adventures of Trimmer Trend and his fellow characters, Simon Slight-Oversight, Tonguely Smoothcheek, Morality Slipping, Doctor Glossover Thinlay, Miles Miss-point etc. This is a pity, because it's a very ingenious play and makes intriguing use of a whole range of comic techniques taken from music hall and radio and television satire, as well as the English mummers plays and the Italian Commedia dell' Arte, in order to put its message across. The plot is simple and straight-forward. Trimmer Trend is the ordinary man of the twentieth century. The author presents him to us as semi-honest and semi-virtuous, always 'reasonable' but never willing to commit himself to the kind of action which he really knows to be right. He is condemned because of his lack of moral courage and pathological addiction to compromise. According to the play he is brought to trial for the murder of his own conscience. The drama has a moral judgment to deliver and does so with tremendous vigour. At some times the principles involved are presented quite openly as embodied ideas without any attempt at a theatrical disguise – for instance there is a personage called 'Conscience', and another representing 'Divorce'; 'Conformity', as might be expected, plays a key role!

It's a very entertaining play and packs a tremendous punch principally because it's hard to believe there's not a good deal of Trimmer in most of us. The things he says and does, the kinds of situation he gets himself into, are all painfully familiar to me, at least! Like most street theatre it depends for its effect on its

contemporary relevance and uses a comic approach to bring home
a serious message.

The serious use of humour is a very ancient technique, of course
(remember Aristophanes and Plautus!) There is humour in the
miracle plays, notably the plays about Noah and the celebrated
Second Shepherd's Play in the Townley cycle. Its purpose is different
here, however. In the miracle plays, humour is used as it is in
Shakespeare's tragedies and history plays, in order to provide a foil
for the serious and tragic passages. There are certainly serious parts
of *Trimmer Trend,* too, but somehow they fail to move us as much
as they do in other more 'conventional' kinds of drama. Plays like
this make their point, and it's often a very good one, very sharp
indeed. But the lack of genuine emotional involvement on our part
blunts the weapon's edge. It pricks and draws blood but it doesn't
cut to the quick. We recognize certain things about ourselves in the
protagonist, but we never really identify with him. In fact the lesson
to be learned from the experience when we compare it with other
kinds of play that we've known is that we tend to identify much
more closely with people who aren't nearly as like ourselves as
Trimmer Trend is! People like Hamlet or Pontius Pilate, or even
Jesus himself! Which is surprising, when you consider how interesting the ideas put forward in the play are, and how successful it is
in convincing us on an intellectual level that this is someone very
like ourselves.

I think the answer lies in the plot. It's what happens to people in
plays that makes us feel for them, and it's only when we feel for
them that we identify ourselves with them. Aristotle calls the plot
'the soul of the drama' – and he's right. A play which really moves
you, really impresses itself on your life, is one which makes you say
'it could be me'. Not 'it's like me', but 'it could be me'. These things
could be happening to me. If the plot is striking enough, if it arouses
our imagination powerfully enough, we will carry ourselves, our
own lives, into the world of the play because we know what it would
be like if it was us, not them. Not him or her, but me. I'm not sure
how this happens but I think it has to do with the interaction between
story and character. My own explanation would be something like
this: We discover what the people in the play are like, not by the
names the author has given them, or even the things that they tell
us about themselves, but by the way they react to what happens in
the story. In this way, character emerges from situation: and in fact

the play is a process of discovery involving both audience and actors. The actor's own understanding of the character's experience develops as he or she becomes more and more immersed in what is happening to them in the story – that is, as they allow themselves to become involved, through their imagination, ever more deeply in the new world that they're helping the dramatist to create. At the same time, and in the same way, exactly the same process is at work in the audience. Like explorers on a voyage of discovery, actors and audience advance together into new territory as the plot unfolds before them. The marvellous thing about this is that it can happen time after time, and in fact does do. The power of focussed imagination is so great that no amount of familiarity can blunt the impact of a particular play, and night after night, century after century, ancient dramas come alive as audiences and players redis-cover the deep emotional truth enshrined in a playwright's original inspiration.

You can see from all this that some kinds of play are really acts of devotion. They call forth a real gift of the self in service of a particular idea about the true meaning and significance of life. If this idea is a religious one, concerning the relationship between God and mankind, such a play may be a way of worshipping God in Spirit and in truth. We offer our willingness to surrender to the play's central message, as this is given a living form by the feelings and thoughts of everyone taking part – whether it be on stage or in the audience – as an act of love to the one who reveals himself to us as the living Word. Other kinds of play use a different kind of approach to the business of getting a religious message across to an audience. Plays like *The Trial of Trimmer Trend* are more 'evangelistic' than 'devotional'; evangelistic in the sense that the word is used in common parlance, to mean a direct attempt to win people over to a stronger and more committed kind of Christian obedience than they had had before. The evangelism of this kind of play is of a robust kind because it is intended for open air performance; it makes you laugh and then it makes you think, perhaps along lines which may be unfamiliar to you if you're not a church member. Its effect may not be quite so great when it is performed actually in church, or in other situations where most of the audiences are practising Christians. It will always amuse and entertain, and provide a starting-point for discussion both among Christians and others; but I always have the feeling when this kind of play is performed within a more formal setting, such as a church or a chapel, of 'preaching to the converted'. For occasions when you're taking the faith out to the people who don't usually give much thought to matters of ultimate concern about the meaning of human behaviour, the format couldn't be bettered.

Plays of this kind, street theatre plays, mount a direct assault upon the audience's sensibilities, using not only actors and actresses, but scenery, props and sound effects, everything that comes to hand, in fact, to make quite sure that no part of the message could possibly be either misinterpreted or ignored. The historical background of this tradition of theatre is a distinguished one. Miracle plays were not the only kind of religious drama in vogue during the Middle Ages. Another kind of theatrical presentation, the morality play, used a more allegorical, less scriptural, approach. Morality plays dealt with timeless truths, absolute virtues and vices, rather than the meaning of certain vital historical happenings which had formed key points in the story of God's purpose for his creation. You could sum this up by saying that whereas the mystery plays told a story, the morality plays preached a sermon. The characters of the moralities are embodied virtues and vices, and their actions on stage are designed to illustrate these characteristics. In fact, they themselves are characteristics rather than true characters. *Characters* are people who live within a particular setting of time and place, men and women whose actions and experiences are not to be distinguished from their *mise-en-scène* of the other folk with whom they have dealings, and the unique events in which they are involved. Real characters are never merely animated ideas. They are personages whose personal identity develops as their situation changes and their story proceeds. They have no identity apart from the story that gives them life – but within that story they have something of the vivid human presence that we experience with regard to the people in our own story. They make the story and the story 'makes' them. (It's all very like life, in fact!) But as far as the mediaeval morality plays go, apart from the central character, the Everyman figure who stands for humanity in general – humanity as an *idea* – it's doubtful whether the play contains anybody 'real' at all; and, of course, as the ideal, or universal, nature of the central figure becomes more and more obvious, so his or her ordinary humanness decreases. These animated allegories present us with a cavalcade of emblems of vice and virtue. They are a moving picture of humanity, often vividly expressive and able to make their point with tremendous impact, but they are never really personal. However much they impress us, they can't involve us. The hero of a morality play tends to remain isolated, surrounded by the highly coloured ghosts of ideas with which he can never make a real relationship, as they aren't people at all, but simply detached parts or aspects of himself. And if *he* can't relate to them, what chance have we?

But this isn't what such plays are really for. The idea isn't to involve us in the world of the plot so that we identify with the characters and learn from their experiences in a way that is genuinely personal – the way we learn from one another in life – but to inform and instruct us about abstract principles. To demonstrate the truth of certain moral and philosophical propositions in the simplest, clearest and least mistakeable way. There's no mystery in the moralities! You don't have to go away and work out the meaning for yourself. Instruction takes place actually *in situ*, as it does in a classroom – and you can't avoid it, either!

For example: In the *Castle of Perseverance*, a fifteenth-century morality play, the actor impersonating Satan is instructed to run around in the audience letting off fire-crackers, which have been specially inserted into all the orifices of his fantastically horrific costume. In this way he demonstrates the impact of demonic chaos on God's world by causing as much actual havoc in as literal a way as he can. Instead of being invited to accept a symbolic representation as a psychological reality in which they are able to participate by using their imagination, the audience is assaulted by a direct frontal attack upon their sensibilities. You aren't just told what is good and bad, right and wrong, angelic or demonic, the knowledge is quite literally beaten into you. You can't miss the point, however hard you try.

For a long time these two kinds of mediaeval theatre existed alongside each other. This isn't really surprising because they represent two basic approaches to the business of putting on plays, and examples of them can be found at every period of history. For instance, during the last twenty years, the totalitarian impulse to batter audiences into subjection has re-emerged very strongly in multi-media presentations which bombard the audience from all sides at once with light, sound and projected images, sometimes surrounding us with the action of a play by staging incidents and provoking 'happenings' at strategic points in the auditorium, or using an acting area which encircles the spectators and allows various episodes of the play to take place simultaneously. As you can imagine, this has a devastating effect on your ability to distinguish fact from fiction and come to your own conclusions about the ideas and attitudes which are being urged upon you.

The main difference between the mystery plays and the moralities wasn't that the former were serious and restrained and the latter unsophisticated and full of violent attacks upon the audience's sensibilities, for the mysteries also had their riotous moments and the morality plays their episodes of thoughtfulness and solemnity. Rather, it was a matter of the play's approach to the task of communicating religious truth to an audience. We have precisely the same problem today. We, too, can decide which way to go about it, the 'mystery way', or the 'morality method'. Whereas in a morality play the actors direct their attention upon the audience, in the mysteries both actors and audience direct their attention upon the play. The play itself provides a kind of metaphorical meeting place for all concerned. In the mysteries, and those plays which, like them, depend on imaginative involvement, communication is mediated rather than directed. In other words, it is *communication-via-communion*. Both kinds of theatre involve ideas as well as feelings; but the object of the morality is to approach these directly (or even fiercely!) while the mystery approach is much more circumspect.

The mystery kind of play sets out to create a world of its own, whereas the morality kind doesn't. To use examples from outside explicitly religious theatre you could say that *Hamlet* creates such a world, but *The Good Woman of Setzuan* does not. It doesn't intend to. The world of *The Good Woman* is quite specifically our own world, and the points that it makes about life, the emotions it arouses in us – valuable, even vital points, powerful and salutory emotions – refer directly to our own situation. Such is Brecht's clearly stated intention. Hamlet's ideas and feelings, on the other hand, primarily concern the stage-world of Elsinore, and reach us at second-hand. That is, he tells us about them and invites us to see them in action. Hamlet's life (and Gertrude's and Claudius's) are ours only by implication, and if we want to understand them in any depth we ourselves must do something about it. In other words, we must go out to meet them. In fact, this isn't very hard to do, if we're only willing to do it, because we perceive their reality as people so intensely that their life reaches out across the barrier of theatrical illusion and beckons us to join them. Theirs is still the first move; we willingly co-operate.

Obviously there's a paradox here. Brecht addresses himself directly to us, while Shakespeare is involved with his characters, and simply allows us to 'get in on the act' if we want to, or are willing to let his characters persuade us. And yet his people are so much more real than Brecht's – real as people, that is, rather than personified ideas. Perhaps the reason for this is that in the theatre, as in life, genuine human relationship happens most strikingly in circumstances where feelings are not forced upon us – situations of 'free association', in fact. The play which is self-contained, a world of its own, a game of make-believe which we are ourselves involved in creating, provides a meeting-place where all sorts of genuine discoveries can be made: discoveries about the underlying truth of human life, the truth which underpins all illusion and artifice, social and personal as well as theatrical. Discoveries about the self and other people and what lies *between*. . . This kind of dramatic experience makes us acknowledge the theatre as a place of truth, where our need to protect ourselves by looking at life in a detached way as if we were not involved – our need for make-believe in fact – is first of all consciously faced, and then actively used to induce a greater involvement, a more whole-hearted gift of self to other. The gap between two kinds of reality, our own world and the play's leads us away from ourselves towards what is not us, but is fascinatingly like us, and could, our heart tells us, actually *be* us! Just give it time, that's all. In the theatre of imaginative involvement we are invited to participate in our own way and at our own speed, protected by the theatrical illusion, yet exposed by the emotional truth of genuine human feelings which we can identify with. We are not actually given explicit instructions to accept, understand, believe, anything. Which is why we end up understanding so much and believing so deeply.

Separation and communion, observing and identifying are partners in the process of understanding, not rivals. Both comedy and tragedy originate in our perception of the relationship between subject and object, as something which can't really be divided. It's always 'me' and 'not-me' *at the same time*. The movement of recoil by which we withdraw to a safe distance in order to contemplate someone else's predicament without becoming involved always seems an inadequate kind of defence. The more we try to keep aloof, the more we get involved. It's as if distance draws us in, makes us feel things more personally. When we set about creating 'aesthetic distance' in the theatre by using a made-up story and peopling it with fictional characters separated from the audience by a raised platform, curtains and stage lighting, we simply give free play to the powerful electricity that flows between us as we focus on what's happening 'before our very eyes'. People who use a shared imaginative experience to convey a message about life should never forget this. It's basic to all kinds of drama. If you want to use a play to communicate the gospel you must always remember that plays aren't sermons. Religious drama works best when it uses the approach taken by Jesus himself, in his parables: I am not *this particular prodigal son,* and understand this well enough; it's only when my imagination leads me to see myself in him, my behaviour in his behaviour, that I take what happens to him in a personal way and use my ears to hear the timeless truth contained in the made-up story. The 'theatre of parable' is the theatre of recognition rather than indoctrination. It sets out to intrigue rather than inform – but because it makes us do the work of interpreting and understanding for ourselves, it ends up imparting the kind of information we simply can't forget. Sometimes this may take a little time, particularly if it's the kind of message we don't really want to receive, or don't want to apply personally to ourselves. Most of us are rather good at not seeing the point of the very things that concern us most deeply. The information takes time to sink in; but when it eventually penetrates to those levels of our mind where the real work of understanding is done it can affect our whole view of the world and ourselves. This is why it's better not to have a public discussion immediately the curtain has fallen. Give it time to work!

On the other hand, there is certainly a place for 'discussion-type theatre' – the kind of play that jolts us into an immediate response by its extrovert approach to communicating ideas that we can't help recognizing as obviously applying directly to *us* and to no one else. I remember a very effective play of this kind which had for its theme the difficulty of making political decisions. The setting of the play, specially chosen in order to exploit all the available possibilities of this particular theme, was an emergent African country in the process of putting together its first constitution. The country had a varied history and contained a number of ethnic groups. Over the years it had formed part of a succession of other states, some colonial, some independent, native to Africa. It also took in various parts of other states which now had to share a new common political identity. As you can see, the opportunities for discord were almost endless! The various political, social and racial and religious factors to be considered were not kept to the actors, but shared among everyone present, to the extent of encouraging various members or groups of members of the audience to align themselves with particular sections of the new community. People spoke up as themselves-as-they-would-feel-in-a-particular-situation, and the outcome of the play depended on how the discussion progressed. There was a good deal of argument, of course, and it was sometimes difficult to keep order; but it was here that the actors' skill came in. Because they had had time to develop and experiment with representative 'characters', and rehearse alternative outcomes for the debate which could be integrated with the overall story line, they were able to control the proceedings and give the event some kind of recognizable shape. They never knew just how a particular performance would end in the sense of what kind of a constitution would finally emerge, because this still remained to a large extent in the hands of the audience, but this was what made the thing so exciting. It really was the audience's play, and the actors were perpetually stimulated by the need to keep on their toes in the effort to decide when to lead and when to follow.

This kind of theatre certainly has a tremendous amount to offer religious drama. At the moment it is still largely unexplored. Perhaps someone reading this book will recognize its possibilities and respond to the challenge. It obviously is a challenge, because any group that undertakes the experiment needs to have the ability to trust more to instinct and inspiration than to the safeguards against disaster provided by orthodox theatrical structure. Most plays are quite explicit about the shape of the event which is to take place. They lay down definite rules about where and when the play is set, how long it will last, what the people in it have to say, and how they're supposed to say it. This, on the other hand, is theatre at its least formal. It isn't really improvization, because the minimal procedural guidelines have been laid down in advance in order to make sure that it still retains its identity as theatre, something intended to be presented to an audience rather than emerging directly from the experience of the group. On the other hand, it certainly is subject to what Goffman calls 'chance selection', and not 'pure' theatre in which the kind of relationship between the play itself and the people watching it is clearly and precisely determined, and woe betide anyone who chances to step out of line!

I've included the play at this point because of the directness of the actors' approach to the audience. People are encouraged to take an active, vocal, part in the proceedings, as they are in pantomimes, and also certain kinds of music-hall acts. The closest example of overtly religious theatre which is in vogue at present are the sketches written by Paul Burbridge and Murray Watts for performing in church or as 'street theatre'. These invariably provoke an immediate response from the audience, and usually lead to animated discussion afterwards. They are extremely witty and make their point with unerring accuracy:

(Narrators One and Two)
Two: Jesus told a story
One: About
Two: A man
One: Who had
Two: Three servants – for the sake of argument:
One: Fred, (Pause while Fred enters and takes up position)
Two: Ted, (Pause while Ted enters and takes up position)
One: And Julian Potterton-Brown. (Longer pause while Julian Potterton-Brown makes a fastidious entrance)
Two: Now Ted was smarter than Fred.
One: But Fred was bigger than Ted
Two: Ted had a head to earn him his bread
One: Which cannot be said for Fred
Two: But Fred often said
One: 'I don't 'ave Ted's 'ead
Two: I manage with muscles instead.'
One: Now Julian Potterton-Brown
Two: Was the odd one out.
One: But this didn't deter him – after all:
Two; 'I'm frightfully well-bred,' he said
One: 'I'm greasier than Ted', he said
Two; 'I'm lazier than Fred', he said
One: 'And I don't rhyme with either of them, the creeps'. etc.

Time to Act, Hodder 1979, p. 24

This is part of a sketch based on Jesus's parable of the talents. It's a sure-fire hit, when it's done well, and greatly to be recommended as a practical, short, contemporary morality. The two books of sketches by Burbridge and Watts contain many minor masterpieces of their genre.

One word of warning, however. Plays like this do take a lot of skill to do well. And they aren't all that successful when they're not. The performance needs to come at least some way up to the writing. You might think, and rightly, that this is true of all plays. However, it's more true of these than most. The sketches contained in these two collections aim at enlightenment through entertainment, and the intention to entertain carries certain responsibilities. In this case it demands the ability to time lines (and parts of lines) well, to pick up cues with professional speed, to undercut and over-ride vocally, to throw lines away, etc. Much of the time you'll find yourself addressing the audience, with nothing to hide behind, no real character to mediate between you and them. So you have to be good! Remember – the less artistic structure for the creation of a 'make-believe' world on stage, the more the play is opened up to the audience, and the harder it is to keep the game of theatre going. If the actors can lose themselves in the play they can take their audience with them so that both actors and audience may find themselves, and one another, at a deeper level than that of 'let's pretend'.

Notes

1. Bertolt Brecht's *The Good Woman of Setzuan* is one of his *Parables for the Theatre*. An edition is published by Penguin (1966).

2. The sociologist Irving Goffman draws an important distinction between various degrees of intensity in the relationship between the complementary roles of participant and spectator, which he grades according to what he calls 'purity of social bond'. The least 'pure' bond is ordinary, self-directed behaviour: 'I live'. The tightest or 'purest' bond, is self-revelation or demonstration: 'I show how life is lived'. Theatre, he maintains, is really very different from less

formal, more spontaneous 'games with rules'. The kind of play I've been describing here would belong in the fifth circle (E) of the diagram he uses to illustrate his idea, rather that the central one (F) (I. Goffman, *Frame Analysis*, Harper and Row 1974).

A Life

B Optional beguilements
   (e.g. party games)

C Situations which some people
   watch (spectator sports)

D Formal demonstrations
   (traditional teaching or
   lecturing)

E Public ceremonies (rituals)

F Theatre

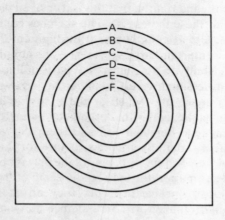

3. Two books of sketches by Paul Burbridge and Murray Watts, *Time to Act* (Hodder 1979) and *Lightening Sketches* (Hodder 1981) are available. The extract from *Time to Act*, copyright © 1979 by Paul Burbridge and Murray Watts, is reprinted by permission of Hodder and Stoughton Ltd. *The Trial of Trimmer Trend* by Murray Watts hasn't been published.

7 What the Building Says

Where you stage a play has a powerful effect on its message. By taking religious drama out of the church building and into the streets and market places of mediaeval Europe, the actors and actresses of the mystery plays vividly proclaimed the meaning of the gospel message to be something which concerns life in society just as much as worship within the sanctuary. In the same way modern Christians are using drama as a metaphor for social man in an age which calls for the redemption of community as desperately as any has done before it. Nowadays, the emphasis is upon multi-media presentations rather than mystery plays, as men and women make the best use of all the facilities available to them for proclaiming their message in as forceful and dramatic a way as possible. A good example of the projection of the Christian message to a community deeply divided on social, religious and racial grounds was the events which took place in Bradford at Eastertide in 1983 (transmitted as part of the BBC's *Songs of Praise* programme on 22 January 1984). The theme of this was the solidarity of the human race in and through Jesus Christ, and the message was proclaimed in sound and light as well as verbally, with the voices of people of all the races and ethnic groups shouting out from every part of the city 'He's risen! He's risen! He's in all the world!' The theme of the New Creation in which there is 'neither Jew nor Greek, slave nor free man' is central to the awareness of Christians in many British cities nowadays, as the following letter to *The Times*, written in 1981, shows so very vividly:

Sir. On the night of Monday April 13th, while violence held sway in Brixton, a multi-racial, multi-denominational crowd of three thousand watched 'The Way of the Cross' enacted in the streets of Notting Hill. Jesus was played by a black youth. There was a multi-racial cast of two hundred. Far from there being violence among the crowd, a spirit of tolerance, harmony and goodwill prevailed throughout the four hours. However, except for a slot on BBC television that night and slight coverage in one or two newspapers the next day, the national media, including your own paper, failed to report this good news. Instead they served the desires of their public faithfully and daily with a newsfare of sensation and fear. . . The drama ended with the Resurrection taking place in a patch of torn ground which is to be transformed into a garden: Death into Life. It was all amazing and worthy of being seen by millions and I cry with sorrow and fury at the absurdity that it was not.

(Enid Williams, quoted by permission)

All for Christ, and Christ for all! The message of such an event – in such a setting – can't possibly be misconstrued.

The process works both ways, however, Just as performing religious drama in the middle of all the noise and violence, strife and tension, of the world instead of within the quietness of a church building has the effect of emphasizing the universal significance of its message, so the religious implications of ordinary 'secular' drama are underlined by presenting it in a church setting.

Whistling Wally is a play for television by Walter Daly. It is set in a working-class district in the North of England, and concerns the relationship between a teenage boy and his father Wally. Wally is dying of cancer. Kevin, the play's central character, is about to depart on a motorcycling holiday with his work-mate, Norm. His father is in hospital, however, and Kevin feels he ought to wait until he has been discharged home again before he sets off for France on the back of Norm's bike. He has a lot of affection for his father and also a good deal of contempt for him, regarding him as a feckless and irresponsible man who spends far too much time and money in the pub. In fact, he is considerably ashamed of him, and can't understand why other people, including his own friend Norm, regard him with respect. He doesn't know that, in fact, Wally has cancer.

When his mother tells him how things really stand – that Wally is dying and has only a short time to live, although he himself has not been told this and expects to get better, Kevin is deeply shocked. His immediate reaction is one of anger on behalf of Wally himself, whom he thinks is being made a fool of by people who refuse to take him seriously. In the play's key scene, Kevin visits Wally in hospital. He discovers that, in fact, his father is very well aware that he is shortly going to die and that his wife and son know this. He, too, has preferred to keep the knowledge to himself because he judges that they will be more distressed than ever if they suspect that he actually knows that he is dying. He doesn't believe in hurting other people simply in order to relieve his own feelings. His words reveal him as a person of great dignity. For the first time in his life, Kevin is impressed by his own father. . .

At Wally's funeral, Kevin is made very angry by the boozy festivities which he sees as the final crowning insult to his father, a man who was underrated when he was alive and is even being made a fool of in death. The violence of his outburst causes his uncle to respond even more violently: 'This is your father's night, not yours. *And you never even knew him.*' Kevin, it turns out, has got it all wrong. It was because his friends and neighbours loved Wally so much that they laughed at him. In fact they laughed at him because they knew that this, above anything else, was what he wanted them to do. They understood, too, that it was for their sake, not his own, that he wanted it. He was 'Whistling Wally', the man who, whatever happened, was always cheerful. They recognized him as a living proof of the impregnability of the human spirit: 'While Wally was happy, there couldn't be much wrong with the world, and pints were a small price to pay for what he gave us.' The play ends with Kevin's departure on his delayed holiday. Before he goes, he tells his mother that, when he gets back, he intends to leave his job in the foundry where his father used to work, and try something more adventurous – the kind of thing his father would have liked to do with his own life, if his main business hadn't been simply that of keeping other people cheerful in the face of adversity. (Kevin doesn't actually say this, however. It is left to the audience to understand, from what has gone before, and from a very moving speech at his father's graveside, in which he accepts the fact that, in fact, he has never seen below the surface of his father's attitude to life, so that it is only in retrospect that he can know the man as he really was; that, for him, things have changed quite drastically, and life will never be the same again. . .)

Although *Whistling Wally* was originally written for television, its author gave us permission to present it in an entirely different setting, and its first performance took place in a large Victorian

church, in the wide space in front of the organ pipes. It was the first
time that a play had been performed there, and we weren't able to
make any kind of attempt at a realistic set. If we could have made
the church really dark, we might perhaps have reproduced the kind
of effect achieved on television by using stage lighting to define a
series of separate acting areas, in which case the absence of scenery
and the comparatively large space available to us could have been
exploited in order to allow one scene to flow easily into the next, as
the author had intended. In St Faith's church, however, we had
neither stage lighting nor black-out material; the evening sun shone
into the building through fifteen immense, plain glass windows, and
we were left to our own devices. These consisted of a hospital bed
improvised out of a kitchen chair and a bench, two more kitchen
chairs, a small table, and our own and the audience's imaginations.

There was a slight difficulty here, as well. Our producer wasn't
used to staging plays under quite such Spartan conditions as these,
and couldn't imagine how such a ramshackle set-up could possibly
induce an audience to suspend its disbelief. She apologized to
them about it all before the play started: understandable in the
circumstances, perhaps, but not exactly guaranteed to increase her
cast's confidence in what was about to take place. The audience
themselves, on the other hand, weren't really looking for an
evening's entertainment, a chance to escape from the pressure of
immediate reality, but had come along in order to assess the play's
message in as clear-headed a way as possible. They were members
of a seminar on Terminal Care and Bereavement, and had been
invited along to see *Whistling Wally* as part of the academic require-
ments of the course – a kind of cross between an animated 'visual
aid' and an exercise in educational role-play. As such, their aim was
criticism rather than collusion. For those of us in the cast, it didn't
look as though it was going to be a very enjoyable evening.

Actually, it was the best performance of the play that we ever
gave. In some strange way, the absence of any attempt at a realistic
set made it easier for us to concentrate on what was happening to
the people we were 'being'. When we had performed the play on
an ordinary stage, with normal stage-lighting, we'd always been
uncomfortably aware that it was constructed in a way that was
authentically televisual, calling for a rapidly flexible style of presentation which couldn't be achieved on stage: not at least on the kind
of stages we had at our disposal. The result was that we fell over

ourselves – often quite literally – in an attempt to reproduce a kind of theatre that was beyond the resources of our particular medium. In St Faith's, we stopped trying to convince ourselves and the audience that we were really on television, and concentrated on doing the play for its own sake. The action went backwards and forwards in time, shifting its location with alarming frequency, but we couldn't disguise the fact that we were forced to represent all that happened within the same spatial and temporal dimensions, leaving it to the audience to determine whereabouts a scene was supposed to be taking place, and disentangle the succession of events within the main story-line from the numerous flash-backs which, however effective they might be on the cinema or on television, on an open stage without scenery or lighting could only have the effect of confusing the issue.

The result was a naturalistic play presented in a way which, so far as its actual staging was concerned, ran entirely counter to the conventions of naturalistic theatre. Even so, it effectively created a world of shared imagination able to hold both actors and audience completely enthralled until the final line. The effect of abandoning the artificial, exterior techniques of stage illusion, with its life-like settings and hypnotic use of light and sound, was to throw both actors and spectators back upon their own resources of imagination, their instinctive response to a story about their fellow human beings, which circumstances had ensured could make only the most minimal claim to be anything other than a story. The realism of the event came from *within:* within the story itself, and within each individual actor and spectator. There in the church, we let our imaginative forces work upon the problem of making emotional and intellectual sense of the things that were happening to the people within the play. In the event, all the things that appeared to stand in the way of a successful performance – the audience's attitude of clinical detachment, the actors' lack of confidence and crippling sense of nakedness at having to act on a bare stage without the realistic scenery and lighting that the play seemed to demand in order to be effective, plus the producer's obvious embarrassment and lack of confidence – all these things proved grist to the mill of the audience's imagination, so that when we finished we were received in the way actors love best of all, the brief, two-second pause for breath before an audience comes back at you with the applause that says so clearly and unambiguously, 'message received and understood'.

All in all, this particular audience stayed breathless for quite some time because the pause began again after the clapping had stopped, so that it seemed like several minutes before people began to talk. When they did, it wasn't in the way we expected. As I said, the intention was to stimulate a discussion about the ways in which the particular people in *Whistling Wally* had behaved in a situation involving the terminal illness of one of the main characters. The kind of question that we expected to be asked was 'should Kevin's mother have told him earlier that Wally had cancer and was almost certainly going to die?'; or 'wouldn't it have been better if Wally and his wife had been able to be honest with each other at this most crucial point in their relationship?' 'Was it really each other they were trying to protect, or could it actually have been themselves?' Perhaps someone might have wanted to open a discussion on the play's central theme, namely the effect of an experience of personal loss in leading to increased self-awareness (for Kevin only begins to understand himself when he discovers how wrong he has been about his father). Nobody said anything about these things.

When eventually the questions started to come, they were questions and comments about the play itself rather than about what the play was about. It had been a very moving experience, people said. They hadn't expected to enjoy it as much as they had done. No, they hadn't been put off by the absence of scenery and lighting. Well, maybe a bit at first, but they'd soon got used to it. When we asked them what they thought about the play *as a play* – did they think that it managed to get its message across? they said, Oh yes, certainly, it had a very powerful impact. It was about death, and about family relationships, two subjects which always have a powerful impact, don't they? We asked them to be more explicit about the nature of the play's message. At this point we drew a blank. They didn't want to talk about abstract things; they wanted to talk about personal experiences instead.

For over an hour we left behind us any desire to draw intellectual conclusions and spoke personally and spontaneously about ourselves. Gradually, the atmosphere in the church grew more intimate as people began to talk about things that they found painful to mention. It was a time for feeling and sharing rather than analysing and reflecting. The play itself was forgotten as we remembered our own private dramas, discovering new things about ourselves as we disclosed ourselves to other people. What had been planned as a cerebral exercise became a personal experience.

Whistling Wally is a play with several messages, most of them quite clearly presented by the play's action. For instance, it shows how we don't really know the very people we think we know best of all, the people closest to us. If we love them, then we may be quite wrong about why we love them (or why, in fact, they deserve our love). It's also a play about how people project their own problems on to others: because Kevin is so unsure of himself, so afraid of not being taken seriously, he feels disgusted by the apparent lack of regard for his father. Thirdly, the play concerns the hidden pride of people who have been wounded by life and have found strength to follow their own way, whatever that may be. Finally, and above all, it's about life and death, life in the presence of death as an inescapable fact, and the way we react by keeping silent before others and before ourselves. On reflection, *Whistling Wally* is about all these things, and probably about other things as well.

On reflection. The performance in St Faith's church was one of the first events in a programme of lectures and discussions which continued for almost a month. Death was only one of the subjects which made up a short residential course for theological students on matters concerning health and wholeness. As the month went on, some of the questions suggested by the play they had seen at the beginning of the course began to emerge in private conversations and public discussions among the students and their teachers. Matters which might seem at first to have no direct or obvious reference to Kevin and Wally were set quite deliberately within the context of ideas drawn from the play. It was as if the play had ceased to be an event possessing emotional implications of a personal nature, and had become an idea to be used, like other ideas, as a way of making intellectual sense of the situations that confront men and women in the world. In other words, it had taken time for the play to have its full effect. The balanced discussion we had planned for the hour immediately after the performance, and which turned out so differently (disappointingly so from the point of view of our immediate intention) did actually happen in the form of a dozen or more exchanges which took place over a period of weeks rather than minutes.

There's no doubt that *Whistling Wally* came over to that particular audience as a profoundly religious play; and this impression grew during the rest of the course. People came to regard the story of Kevin and Wally as a parable of redemption through vicarious suffering: the son comes to know the father through the latter's patient suffering, and is spiritually changed, discovering his own 'courage to be' in the experience of putting himself emotionally at risk on behalf of someone else. From their comments during the rest of the course it became apparent that this audience had actually seen a play about the danger of spiritual pride and the need for humility and self-understanding. Some of them, who were psychologically as well as theologically inclined, talked about 'ontological insecurity' and the need for 'self-disclosure': but they meant precisely the same thing! Had the author himself been present, he might well have said that this was not the play he had written at all, for he had had no intention of writing theology or Christian doctrine. He would probably have said that they were entitled to interpret his work in that way if they so wished; he might even have gone so far as to admit that *Whistling Wally* does in fact lend itself particularly well to such an interpretation; but he would almost certainly not have used the words that they used. Most authors prefer to let their work speak for itself. He might even have said, like Ernest Hemingway, that if they wanted a message, they should 'try Western Union'!

There is no doubt at all, however, that *Whistling Wally* can be legitimately interpreted in a Christian way, and that it contains 'Christianity in solution'. To this extent it can be considered to be religious theatre. But so can a very great number of plays if they're looked at 'with the eye of faith'. Any play which treats human relationships with sensitivity and compassion will remind a Christian of his deepest feelings about the meaning of life and death; will in fact speak to him about God. It has to be stressed that this particular play wasn't in any explicit sense concerned with mankind's relationship with God. It never actually mentions God at all in the text. What's more, nobody who saw it on other occasions when we performed it ever mentioned God in connection with it. To them it was a play about family relationships in general and working-class life in particular. And even the theological students only discovered God in it later on, when they'd really thought and felt about it.

I suppose that we actually handed the theological interpretation to them on a plate when we decided to do it in church. At the time, the experience was personal and emotional; the play was something that had happened to them. Later on, it was to be remembered as something that had happened to them *in church*. When we performed the same play in a theatre the reaction was, as I say, quite different. Which leads me to believe that it wasn't really the play at all, but the setting in which it was presented, that had such a profoundly spiritual impact. Or rather, it was the play plus the setting. This is what provided so moving a testimony about Christ's presence in the world of human relationships. In such circumstances any good, truthful play about human joy and suffering would have turned out the same way. To this extent, plays done in churches can't help but be 'religious'.

There was more to it than this, though. *Whistling Wally* is very good theatre. It's also good theatre of a particular kind: realistic drama which invites a high level of imaginative participation on the audience's part. This kind of theatre needs time to sink in, but when it has done it leaves an indelible impression. In this case a play which wasn't intentionally religious acquired a theological significance for a particular kind of audience who had seen it in a particular setting, after a pause for thought. Emotion was recollected in tranquility; *Whistling Wally* made people feel before it made them think. An explicitly theological play, one which sets out to use theatrical characters to demonstrate religious concepts would no doubt have provoked more discussion of an overtly theological kind as soon as the curtain had fallen – if there had been a curtain. In time, however, this play made its audience both think and feel. More than this, although it was delayed, its message eventually had a greater impact than it would have done if it hadn't required any kind of interpretation, any translation of feeling into thought. Precisely because it required minimal interpretation (its message being already so well known) the kind of explicitly religious morality-type play described earlier would not have had anything like the same lasting effect on the audience. This was a play that appeared religious to religious people and particularly so when they saw it performed in church. But because its presentation of human relationships was realistic and convincing the scope of interpretation it offered to an audience was actually almost unlimited. In fact it was restricted only by the number of individual philosophies of life and death represented in a particular audience. For example, because of its industrial proletarian setting, it could have been seen by a Marxist as hard Left Wing propaganda; because the role of the family priest in Wally and Kevin's drama was somewhat peripheral, although this was a Roman Catholic household, an atheistic humanist among the audience might in retrospect have assumed that the point of the play was the impotence of organized religion! In fact there could have been any number of versions of the same original, with the entire process almost outside the author's control, for merely by showing life at all he had put himself at the mercy of the basic need of human beings to interpret life and cling to their own ways of doing so.

So you can see that the play itself and the church building containing it present us with two distinct themes which each of us may choose to harmonize in his or her particular way. That is, if the play itself and the way it's presented leave us any freedom in the matter. I don't mind admitting that I think they should do this, and that plays which allow this kind of freedom are ones which enshrine the true spirit of the drama. To restrict theatre to the business of transmitting a particular message about life in as precise and unmistakeable a way as possible – to spell out a specific religious, philosophical or political doctrine – is to reduce the emotional impact of the theatrical experience so drastically that it hardly seems worth while to stage plays at all. Much better to write broadsheets or preach sermons or stick posters on walls. If the theatre is to be used to extend human understanding, then it should be used in the way that best accords with its own intrinsic nature, as a place of immediate encounter which makes no demands on the way in which we ourselves shall choose to interpret the significance of that encounter. Religious people who write, produce and act in plays must be willing to allow them to be misinterpreted by non- or anti-religious people, in order that the hearts and minds of the favourably disposed may be reached and touched by a powerful experience of human relationship from which they can draw their own theological conclusions. In this way the quality of religious awareness is changed and deepened, and theatre is allowed to be itself and to speak to men and women in its own kind of language, the language of pregnant images rather than logical argument. The fact that we can and do interpret all serious plays – all plays which are seriously intended – in the light of our own personal way of looking at the world, greatly enlarges the scope of plays which can be regarded as suitable for presentation in church. In this century alone, there is the work of Eliot, O'Neill, even Tennessee Williams, writers concerned with the ultimate significance of personal relationships and the moral nature of reality; there are plays about the paradox of personal identity by Pirandello; Genet and Ionesco explore the strange hidden life of the psyche, while the surface patterns of social life reveal hidden harmonies and discords in the plays of writers as varied as Giraudoux and Anouilh, Alan Ayckbourn and Noel Coward; Becket, Miller, and Sartre attempt to reflect ultimate meanings in the mirror of artistic form. All this is religious, if we will have it so. It is religious *for us*.

This isn't all that's to be said, however. There's much more to the religious significance of the drama than the rather commonplace idea that religiously inclined people are likely to interpret the world and everything in it in the light of a particular set of principles drawn from their own theological understanding of life. Genuine drama is *intrinsically* religious. The fundamental principle upon which it depends is a theological one. It is the principle of the relationship of persons, the free encounter of selves which bestows freedom on others. In the theatre we see ourselves as other people, and other people as ourselves. The fundamental unity of human beings is disclosed to us in its authentic nature as unity-in-separation, so that our own individuality is made authentic by the very same movement of soul which acknowledges our dependence on others for our very being. The action of withdrawing into myself in order to be me, to experience my own selfhood, to think my own thoughts and feel my own feelings, is the reflection of the action whereby I am able to give myself to the other person in the moment of encounter, the impulse of a sympathetic fusion with the being who is not I. These two movements of the soul are complementary; that is, they depend on each other for their existence. Theologically speaking, they represent the life of beings who were created in order to give and receive love, and who participate in the Being of God himself, the life which flows freely between persons.

When the matter of art is the living presence of men and women, as it is in the theatre, its significance as a symbol of human relationship is particularly striking. But this is only so where the transaction is a free one, and we are not forced to receive a particular message as the only way in which facts are to be understood and events interpreted. As we saw when we were considering the 'theatre of parable', in order for art to be the symbol of relationship, we must be permitted to withdraw from the encounter and think about what has happened to us in our own way and in our own time. We must be allowed to preserve our independence in order to be truly free to give ourselves away to the other in love. The kind of theatre which limits our freedom to do this may be called 'religious', certainly: but can it be *truly* religious?

As obedience depends on the freedom to disobey, so understanding involves being left at liberty to reject the message offered to us. Just as we can't compel love, we can't force acceptance of the things we stand for. Jesus speaks in parables 'so that seeing they may (be at liberty not to) see, and hearing they may (choose not to) understand'; and he adds, 'He who has ears to hear let him hear'. Let him, don't try and force him! Our acceptance must be genuinely our own; and it must be genuine acceptance. This means that it must be particular and specific, rooted in actual examples of behaviour and experience: He who, *because he has done and suffered these things,* has ears to hear, let him hear *this.* . . He who is ready to receive this particular message at this particular point in his life. . .

The kind of understanding that the gospel demands is more than the intellectual acknowledgment that something or other is true in theory. It is the deep personal acceptance of a spiritual reality as something which is overwhelmingly true of ourselves. There are areas of life where the effort to instil real understanding by means of explanation and exhortation is misapplied and even counter-productive. In the things concerning our profoundest level of awareness – matters of life and death, what things *are* rather than what they're *about* – we're conscious of a kind of 'instruction-gap', a chronic failure to learn in any other way than by our own sufferings and joys. In these vital areas of life, drama plays a unique role by enabling us to use our precious gifts of empathy and imagination to share something of the reality of other people's living experience and to discover for ourselves truths that cannot be communicated in any other way.

Notes

Martin Buber's book *Pointing the Way* (Routledge 1957) contains the best theological description I have ever come across of the relationship which exists between actors and audience in the theatre. The most relevant chapter is the one called 'The Space Problem of the Stage'. See also Chapter 2 of Peter Brook's masterly book *The Empty Space,* MacGibbon and Kee 1968.

Amateur nights for *Whistling Wally* by Walter Daly are handled by Pauline Baker, 2 Margravine Gardens, London W6.